COLUMNBIA COLLEGE

3 2711 00021 5209

D1787470

808.7 B496a   MAY

Berger, Arthur Asa, 1933-

The art of comedy writing

The Art of Comedy Writing

The Art of Comedy Writing

**Arthur
Asa
Berger**

COLUMBIA COLLEGE LIBRARY
600 S. MICHIGAN AVENUE
CHICAGO, IL 60605

TRANSACTION PUBLISHERS
New Brunswick (U.S.A.) and London (U.K.)

808.7 B496a

Berger, Arthur Asa, 1933–

The art of comedy writing

Copyright © 1997 by Transaction Publishers, New Brunswick, New Jersey 08903.

All rights reserved under International and Pan-American Copyright Conventions. No part of this book may be reproduced or transmitted in any form or by any means, electronic or mechanical, including photocopy, recording, or any information storage and retrieval system, without prior permission in writing from the publisher. All inquiries should be addressed to Transaction Publishers, Rutgers—The State University, New Brunswick, New Jersey 08903.

This book is printed on acid-free paper that meets the American National Standard for Permanence of Paper for Printed Library Materials.

Library of Congress Catalog Number: 97-6163
ISBN: 1-56000-324-3
Printed in the United States of America

Library of Congress Cataloging-in-Publication Data

Berger, Arthur Asa, 1933–
   The art of comedy writing / Arthur Asa Berger.
     p. cm.
   Includes bibliographical references and index.
   ISBN 1-56000-324-3 (alk. paper)
    1. Wit and humor—History and criticism. I. Title.
PN6147.B476   1997
808.7—dc21   97-6163
                                                                         CIP

Contents

	Preface	vii
	Acknowledgements	ix
1.	Comic Techniques in Dramatic Comedies	1
2.	The Braggart Captain: *Miles Gloriosus*	51
3.	Make What You Will of Comedy: *Twelfth Night*	65
4.	No Trusting to Appearances: *The School for Scandal*	83
5.	The Devices of Absurdity: *The Bald Soprano*	97
6.	Beyond Devices	111
	Bibliography	119
	Name Index	123
	Subject Index	125

Preface

This little book is not designed to take the joy out of your life or to prevent you from ever laughing again. If it has that effect, and you find that you are unable to laugh without numbers or strange terms (to be explained later) popping into your head, please forgive me.

I didn't mean to destroy your sense of humor. A thousand pardons. It was an unfortunate accident.

What *The Art of Comedy Writing* does is show you how comedy writers create and have created humor. My argument is relatively simple; I claim that there are forty-five techniques (no fewer, no more) that comedy writers and all humorists have used, do use, and must use—to generate humor.

The book will be of use to anyone interested in humor. It is meant to help playwrights, television writers, novelists, film scriptwriters, and stand-up comics who want to create humorous material. It will be of use to anyone who wants to be funny or create humorous material for whatever purpose. In addition, it will be useful to scholars from many disciplines and others who like humor and are curious about how it is created.

If you know how writers and comedians create humor, you can study and analyze the humorous works they have created. For example, you can use the techniques to see how Shakespeare evolved as a comedy writer—or Neil Simon, or whoever strikes your fancy.

You can use the list of forty-five techniques for sociological investigations of what kind of humor Americans, Germans, Japanese, or members of any culture or subculture like (that is, which of the techniques tend to be the dominant ones they use and prefer).

I have used these techniques for a number of years in teaching courses in comedy writing at San Francisco State University and know, from experience, that writers can learn to apply these techniques and adapt them for various purposes—whether it be a play, a monologue, or a humorous radio or television commercial.

These techniques work!

And I've found that when my students learn these techniques, they are able to write some excellent scripts. There is one requirement: if you are going to use these techniques, you've got to have a sense of humor. Let me offer an analogy. I recently watched a marvelous television documentary on Flamenco dancing. The dance teacher said "...there is one fundamental requirement. If you want to be a Flamenco dancer, you've got to have a sense of rhythm. If you don't have rhythm, no amount of teaching can turn you into a good Flamenco dancer."

The same applies to comedy writing. If you don't have a good sense of humor, if you don't like to laugh (and don't have the desire to make other laugh), if you don't have a feel for the absurdities of life, if you don't have a comic sensibility—I don't think this book will help you learn how to write good comedy or analyze humor very well.

But if you do have a sense of the ridiculous, you can learn how some of the greatest writers of comedies have generated humor in their plays. The first chapter of *The Art of Comedy Writing* lists the forty-five techniques of humor and offers examples of how various playwrights have used these techniques.

I make use of material from many playwrights—Plautus, William Shakespeare, Ben Jonson, Oscar Wilde, Samuel Beckett, Tom Stoppard, Trevor Griffiths, and Eugene Ionesco. In the four chapters that follow, I analyze four classic comedies (from Roman comedies to the theater of the absurd) in an effort to show that my forty-five technique are not confined to modern works or any particular style of writing plays.

I believe this book uniquely offers writers and those interested in humor in general an anatomy of the techniques of humor and provides writers and critics with a sizable repertoire of techniques they can use in their work. I see this book being used in courses in creative writing, comedy, and humor in literature departments, writing departments, communications departments, broadcasting and media departments, humanities departments—wherever there is an interest in humor and in the creative process.

Acknowledgements

I would like to express my grateful appreciation to the following publishers who were kind enough to allow me to quote from plays they published: Grove/Atlantic, Inc. for Eugene Ionesco's *The Bald Soprano*, Tom Stoppard's *Travesties*, and Samuel Beckett's *Krapp's Last Tape*, and to Faber & Faber for Tom Stoppard's *Travesties* and Trevor Griffiths's *Comedians*.

1

Comic Techniques in Dramatic Comedies

When we analyze literary works (or in the current jargon "texts") we use the term "style" to represent what is distinctive and personal in an author's writing. We sometimes use the word "voice" to stand for the same thing. In the great authors, this style or voice is often easily recognizable; it has to do with how authors use language, with the tone authors adopt, and with the way authors infuse their philosophy and knowledge about life into their works.

There is also what might be described as "comedic style," namely the techniques an author tends to use to generate laughter. In order to determine comedic style, then, we have to know something about the techniques of humor—which is the subject of this chapter. I will return to this subject shortly, after I discuss a related matter—personal and social style.

On Personal Style and Other Styles

One sign of a distinctive style or voice involves the ease by which an author can be parodied. Thus Hemingway, whose style is very distinctive, is often parodied and there are yearly contests in which Hemingway parodies are awarded prizes. If authors cannot be parodied, it would suggest that there is not much that is distinctive in their writing style.

But there are other styles of writing that are not personal but social, public, or generic. In *Exercises in Style* Raymond Queneau, the brilliant French author took a story that he made up, about a young man taking a bus, and retold that story using something like sixty different styles. Let me quote a few lines from a sampling of his styles.

Double Entry Style
Towards the middle of the day and at midday I happened to be on and got on the platform and balcony at the back of an S-line and of a Contrescarpe-Champeret bus and passenger transport....

Official Letter Style

I beg to advise you of the following facts of which I happened to be the equally impartial and horrified witness. Today, at roughly twelve noon, I was present on the platform of a bus which was proceeding up the rue de Courcelles....

Cross-Examination Style

—At what time did the 12.23 P.M. S-line bus proceeding in the direction of the Porte de Champerret arrive on that day?
—At 12:38 P.M.
—Were there many people on the aforesaid S bus?
—Bags of 'em....

What Queneau's ingenious exercise demonstrates is that there are, in fact, a large number of distinctive styles of "public" writing that we use, depending upon the circumstances. (Queneau's book is, let me suggest, actually a brilliant example of a humorous technique, "theme and variation.") Writers may use a number of different styles depending upon what they are writing and who their audience is.

You don't use the same style when you are writing to a loved one that you use when you are writing to the Internal Revenue Service. Some of the more common styles are: legalistic, paradoxical, exclamatory, mystical, metaphoric, ideological, biblical, absurdist, technological, telegraphic, slangy, and rap. And characters in plays distinguish themselves and gain a sense of identity by the way they speak and the style of language they adopt, which varies from scene to scene in some cases.

On Comic Techniques

Just as there are different styles one can adopt in writing, there are also a number of techniques one can use in generating humor in texts. I have developed a typology of techniques of humor, reproduced in the chart below (taken from my book *An Anatomy of Humor*) that lists forty-five different techniques or devices humorists of all sorts—comedians, novelists, cartoonists, playwrights—use to create humor. This chart is based on a content analysis I made in which I examined examples of humor of all kinds—joke books, plays, comic books, novels, short stories, comic verse, essays and anything else I could get my hands on. I elicited from this sample forty-five techniques that are, I suggest, the basis of humor.

I would argue that every humorous work uses these techniques in various permutations and combinations. We can, for example, analyze jokes and find a number of them at work. And we can look at plays and see how playwrights use these techniques, many times in combination as well, to create funny situations and amuse audiences. When I assembled these techniques I found, also, that they fit under four basic categories:

1. humor involving *identity;*
2. humor involving *language*;
3. humor involving *logic* (and a fourth category that I'm not completely satisfied with)
4. humor involving *action* or *visual* phenomena.

These techniques are listed and discussed below, in alphabetical order, along with their categories, in parentheses. I assume that most of them are more or less self-explanatory, though I will briefly explain how I interpret each term, and in most cases, offer examples. I would argue that the choice an author makes of the techniques and the way an author uses them allow us to define an author's style with much more precision than was possible before.

In the second part of the book I discuss the techniques in chapters devoted to four plays: Plautus's *Miles Gloriosus*, Shakespeare's *Twelfth Night*, Sheridan's *The School for Scandal*, and Ionesco's *The Bald Soprano*. (I use a number of selections from these plays in the first chapter as well—so there is a certain amount of duplication here and there.) My chart listing the forty-five techniques of humor is shown below.

Categories and Techniques of Humor

LANGUAGE	LOGIC	IDENTITY	ACTION
Allusion	Absurdity	Before/After	Chase
Bombast	Accident	Burlesque	Slapstick
Definition	Analogy	Caricature	Speed
Exaggeration	Catalogue	Eccentricity	
Facetiousness	Coincidence	Embarrassment	
Insults	Comparison	Exposure	
Infantilism	Disappointment	Grotesque	
Irony	Ignorance	Imitation	
Misunderstanding	Mistakes	Impersonation	
Over literalness	Repetition	Mimicry	
Puns, Wordplay	Reversal	Parody	
Repartee	Rigidity	Scale	
Ridicule	Theme/Variation	Stereotype	
Sarcasm	Unmasking		
Satire			

Let me point out a number of things about this list:

1. I recognize that I have listed as techniques satire and parody, which many critics see as styles or genres rather than techniques and this causes problems. But I think we can argue that since, in common parlance, we talk about authors satirizing and parodying, it isn't too much of a liberty to describe them as techniques.
2. Techniques are generally found in combination. An insult, which I list as a technique, is not in itself humorous; it is only when the insult is combined with other humorous techniques such as exaggeration, sarcasm, ridicule, etc. that it can be seen as funny. It is sometimes difficult to separate the techniques, or decide which technique is being used, but I believe that with a bit of effort we can do so.
3. Many of the techniques can be reversed. Thus insult humor, when turned on oneself, becomes victim humor, and exaggeration, when reversed, becomes understatement.
4. In some cases, when a number of techniques are being used at the same time, it is difficult to determine which technique is dominant and most applicable to a given bit of dialogue or scene in a text. But I have found, in working with students in classroom exercises, that it is generally possible to decide which technique is dominant and which techniques are secondary in jokes and other texts.
5. These techniques tell what *makes* people laugh. They do not tell us *why* people laugh or find something humorous. That is a subject about which there is a great deal of controversy, and which I will not deal with. You will find that these forty-five techniques have been used by everyone from Plautus to Tom Stoppard—that is, from ancient times to the present day. I also believe that they are universal. One culture might use exaggeration and another understatement, but if a joke or play elicits laughter from people, regardless of where we find the joke or play, it uses certain combinations of the forty-five techniques.
6. We must assume a "play frame" in dealing with these techniques. Insults, for example, are not funny—except in a play frame where make-believe, fantasy and imagination are part of the situation.
7. I have taken my examples from dramatic comedies of all kinds, but each example is somewhat decontextualized. I have pulled out each example of a technique from the scene in which it is found, and thus the examples I use lose something, since we don't know much about the characters involved or what is happening in the plot. I try to supply some context to make the passages more understandable. Also, some of the quotes are rather extensive, to provide a sense of what the characters are like. But the examples, even if they are not always funny in themselves, enable us to see a technique in operation. In the second part of the book, I deal with

four plays in some detail and consider their plots as well as the various techniques they employ.
8. In principle, just as we can use the techniques to analyze humor, we can use them to create humor and that, I suggest, is what playwrights do when they write comedies—though, of course, they do not know about my list of forty-five techniques. But they do know, one way or another, some of these techniques and use them, either consciously or intuitively—or, at times, in some combination of both.

With these considerations in mind, let us look at the forty-five techniques of humor that, in various permutations and combinations, I suggest, are the basis of humor. I will be using these techniques to demonstrate, as precisely as I can, how some of our greatest playwrights generated their humor, though I will mention other things as well, such as plot, theme and characterization.

In the chart that follows, I will list these techniques in alphabetical order and then, in varying degrees of detail, discuss them and show examples of them at work in a number of dramatic comedies.

Techniques of Humor in Alphabetical Order

1. Absurdity
2. Accident
3. Allusion
4. Analogy
5. Before/After
6. Bombast
7. Burlesque
8. Caricature
9. Catalogue
10. Chase Scene
11. Coincidence
12. Comparison
13. Definition
14. Disappointment
15. Eccentricity
16. Embarrassment
17. Exaggeration
18. Exposure
19. Facetiousness
20. Grotesque
21. Ignorance
22. Imitation
23. Impersonation
24. Infantilism
25. Insults
26. Irony
27. Literalness
28. Mimicry
29. Mistakes
30. Misunderstanding
31. Parody
32. Puns
33. Repartee
34. Repetition
35. Reversal
36. Ridicule
37. Rigidity
38. Sarcasm
39. Satire
40. Scale, Size
41. Slapstick
42. Speed
43. Stereotypes
44. Theme/Variation
45. Unmasking

1. *Absurdity, Confusion, and Nonsense (logic)*

This involves playing around with logic (as in *The Bald Soprano*), having fantastic characters who utter seemingly ridiculous statements, and works generally characterized by nonsense and confusion.

6   The Art of Comedy Writing

> MR. SMITH: Here's a thing I don't understand. In the newspapers they always give the age of deceased persons but never the age of the newly born. It doesn't make sense.
>
> MRS. SMITH: I never thought of that.

Here we see one of the many places in *The Bald Soprano* where Ionesco plays around with logic. If newspapers give the age of people who die in obituaries, why don't they give the age of babies who are born in birth announcements? On the face of it, it seems logical, except that we all know the age of babies when they are born. There is also the famous scene where the doorbell rings, but when one of the characters, Mrs. Smith, goes to answer it, there's nobody there. The third time this happens she refuses to answer the door.

> [*The doorbell rings again.*]
>
> MR. SMITH: Goodness, someone is ringing. There must be someone there.
>
> MRS. SMITH: [*in a fit of anger*]: Don't send me to open the door again. You've seen that it was useless. Experience teaches us that when one hears the doorbell ring it is because there is never anyone there.

It is this kind of playing around with logic that I have in mind when I characterize absurdity as a technique of humor. I see a difference between absurdity and infantilism, which I see as involving sounds of words and which sometimes is used to help generate absurdity.

2. *Accident (logic)*

Accidents involve things like slips of the tongue, typographic errors that are amusing, people slipping on banana peels, and that kind of thing. There is a difference between accidents, which are based on chance, and errors or mistakes, which are based on imprudence or ignorance.

There is a scene in Tom Stoppard's *Travesties* which takes place in a library. Tristan Tzara, the Dadaist, has taken a Shakespeare sonnet and cut it into slips of paper, with each slip containing one word. He puts these slips into a hat, which, it turns out later, happens to belong to James Joyce. When Joyce leaves the library he takes his hat with him and, we discover, after leaving, puts it on...without looking in it. All the slips shower down on Joyce and stick to him. The scene follows:

> JOYCE: Rise, sir, from that semi-recumbent posture!
>   (TZARA *and* GWEN *spring apart.* JOYCE *walks across to the main door, picking up his hat, opens the door, addresses* TZARA.) Your monocle is in the wrong eye.

> (TZARA *has indeed placed his monocle in the wrong eye. He replaces it.* JOYCE *has left on his line.*)
>
> GWEN: I must tell Henry!
> TZARA: Have you ever seen my magazine "Dada" darling?
> GWEN: Never, da-da darling!
> (GWEN *kisses him and runs into Henry's room.*)
> (TZARA *starts reading the manuscript in the folder.*)(*The main door opens again and* JOYCE *re-enters, pausing in the threshold. He is covered from head to breast in little bits of white paper, each bit bearing one of the words of Shakespeare's eighteenth sonnet, i.e.* TZARA *was using Joyce's hat. The effect must be immediate and self-evident.*)

We have what turns out to be a mistake by Tzara (using Joyce's hat) and a comic accident, in which Joyce gets covered with white slips of paper that stick to him and make him, for the moment, very comical.

3. *Allusion (language)*

Allusion is a very common technique of humor. Allusions often direct our attention to stupid things people have done, to scandals, to famous sexual liaisons (or to sex in general). One of the problems with understanding comedies from other cultures is that we don't "get" the allusions. The play is a *figure* and the society in which it is found is a *ground* and if we don't know this *ground* we miss a great deal of the humor. In Aristophanes, for example, there are countless allusions to people and events that modern readers do not recognize or understand.

In Stoppard's *Travesties*, there's a scene in which Henry Carr, the lead character, gives a very long speech describing Joyce, Lenin, and Tzara—the three characters who, by chance, are all together in Switzerland and are using the same library. In his description of Tzara, Carr makes an allusion to a well known song, "My Heart Belongs to Daddy."

> CARR: and across the way at Number One, the Meierei Bar, crucible of anti-art, cradle of Dada!!! Who? What? Whatsisay Dada?? You remember Dada!—historical halfway house between Futurism and Surrealism, twixt Marinetti and Andre Breton, 'tween the before-the-war-to-end-all-wars years and the between-the-wars years—*Dada!*—down with reason, logic, causality, coherence, tradition, proportion, sense and consequence, my art belongs to Dada 'cos Dad 'e treats me so—well then....

We have here both wordplay and allusion, as Stoppard plays with the similar sounds of art and heart and dada and daddy and calls to mind a famous song.

8   The Art of Comedy Writing

4. *Analogy, Metaphor (logic)*

Analogies are comparisons and comic analogies are ones that usually involve insult or ridicule. Metaphors and similes are common forms of figurative language that use analogies. Analogies by themselves are not humorous; they must be combined with other techniques of humor such as insults and exaggeration to generate laughter.

For example, in a famous scene in *Volpone*, Mosca is showing Corvino how near death Volpone (supposedly) is. Volpone is pretending to be dying and it is understood that he will leave all his money to whomever it is that is in his favor. A number of people attempt to gain Volpone's favor by giving him gifts. One of these people is Corvino. Mosca, Volpone's servant, is showing Corvino how close to death Volpone is and shouts insults in his ear:

> MOSCA: The pox approach and add to your diseases,
> If it would send you hence the sooner, sir,
> For, your incontinence, it hath deserved it
> Thoroughly and thoroughly, and the plague to boot.
> You may come near, sir—Would you would once close
> Those filthy eyes of yours, that flow with slime
> Like two frog-pits; and those same hanging cheeks,
> Covered with hide instead of skin—Nay, help, sir—
> That look like frozen dish-clouts set on end.
>
>   (*Volpone*, act 1, scene 5)

We see, here, analogies and insults combined together, to create a humorous effect. There is also the matter of imitation (Volpone pretending to be a dying man) and exposure (when Volpone is discovered to be a fraud) at work in the play, topics that will be discussed later in this chapter. And there may be, underneath, a revelation of Mosca's true feelings about Volpone—since at the end of the play Mosca turns on Volpone and steals his fortune.

5. *Before and After: Transformation, Development (identity)*

The technique I've called "before and after" deals with the transformations one often finds in humorous texts. In some cases an inept person is transformed into a sophisticated winner who triumphs over those who had previously made him or her a ridiculous figure. The changes (including the process by which the person is taught to be masterful) and what

Comic Techniques in Dramatic Comedies 9

these changes lead to are the source of the humor. Or, a "winner" is transformed into an inept and defeated figure.

It is difficult to show this technique in a short passage, but there is a decent enough example to be found in Sheridan's *The School for Scandal*. Sir Peter Teazle is talking about his marriage to Lady Teazle.

> SIR PETER: When an old bachelor marries a young wife, what is he to expect? 'Tis now six months since Lady Teazle made me the happiest of men—and I have been the most miserable dog ever since! We tift a little going to church, and fairly quarreled before the bells had done ringing. I was more than once nearly choked with gall during the honeymoon, and had lost all comfort in life before my friends had done wishing me joy...
>
> (*The School for Scandal*, act 1, scene 2)

We get a better idea of what Sir Peter is like a short while later during a conversation with a friend.

> ROWLEY: Come, come, Sir Peter, you love her, notwithstanding your tempers don't exactly agree.
>
> SIR PETER: But the fault is entirely hers, Master Rowley. I am, myself, the sweetest-tempered man alive, and hate a teasing temper; and so I tell her a hundred times a day.
>
> ROWLEY: Indeed!
>
> SIR PETER: Ay; and what is very extraordinary, in all our disputes she is always in the wrong!
>
> (*The School for Scandal*, act 1, scene 2)

Sir Peter is a *senex* figure, an older man who finds that being involved with a younger woman can be very problematic. In many comedies, a senex figures wishes to marry a young woman and plots to do so, but is foiled by the love interests of the woman.

6. *Bombast (language)*

Inflated language and rhetorical exuberance are the basis of bombast. The difference between what is said and the way it is said is one of the reasons we find bombast amusing. Another involves the skill of the person in using this inflated language.

Here is an example from *Volpone* in a scene where he is playing a mountebank, Scoto of Mantua, and is speaking to Celia, Corvino's beautiful wife:

VOLPONE: Here is a poulder concealed in this paper which, if I should speak to the worth, nine thousand volumes were but as one page, that page as a line, that line as a word: so short is this pilgrimage of man, which some call life, to the expressing of it. Would I reflect on the price? Why, the whole world were but as an empire, that empire as a province, that province as a bank, that bank as a private purse to the purchase of it. I will, only, tell you: it is the poulder that made Venus a goddess (given her by Apollo), that kept her perpetually young, cleared her wrinkles, firmed her gums, filled her skin, colored her hair....

(*Volpone*, act 2, scene 2)

The language here is lyrical, elevated and exuberant, though there is also a comic aspect to it in the description of how the poulder helps get rid of wrinkles and firms one's gums. It is the disparity between the elevated language of bombast and its subject that generates the humor.

Our next subject, *burlesque*, is perhaps the most problematic in this typology, since it is a very broad and amorphous one and is used to cover a number of different techniques, each of which has its own identity. Burlesque also refers to a kind of entertainment (at burlesque houses) that features striptease dancers and comedians who tell ribald and often crude jokes and participate in generally stupid and sophomoric humorous skits.

7. *Burlesque (identity)*

Burlesque refers to any literary form that makes individuals, social behavior or other literary works ridiculous by imitating them in an incongruous manner. It is a generic term that covers *satire* (which mocks society), *travesty* (which treats elevated literary works in a low manner) and *lampoon* (which ridicules some individual).

I have included satire as a technique and consider travesty and lampoon as both subsumed under other techniques such as ridicule and insult.

8. *Caricature (identity)*

Caricatures are drawings or other visual art forms in which a person's face is drawn in an exaggerated manner (yet the resemblance is kept) for the purpose of ridiculing the individual. Caricature is often used in political cartoons. Sir Thomas Browne wrote, in 1690, "When men's faces are drawn with resemblance to some other animals, the Italian's call it to be drawn in Caricaturia."

I distinguish between *impersonation*, when one pretends to be someone else (or, in some cases, to have a profession without the requisite training); *imitation*, when one pretends to be something else (or, in Volpone's case, in a different state of being, namely dying); *caricature*, which exaggerates certain aspects of an individual or entity but involves no pretense; and *mimicry*, in which one ridicules someone else by adopting someone else's voice, mannerisms, style of speaking, and so on.

The term caricature is usually used for comic drawings that exaggerate a person's features but maintain a resemblance, but it also can be used in portrayals that do the same thing. Although they are similar, I think it is possible to distinguish between caricature and mimicry.

9. *Catalogues (logic)*

I use the term catalogue to involve lists that can use insult, wordplay, facetiousness and other techniques to obtain humorous effects. This listing or cataloging can be incorporated into dialogue in which a character lists things in response to questions from other characters; the random or incongruous nature of the items listed help create the humor.

Here's a wonderful catalogue from *Volpone* that also uses double-talk and exaggeration. Volpone is pretending to be Scoto Manuano, a seller of health remedies. He describes his "unguento" as something that can "disperse all malignant humors" as follows:

> VOLPONE: To fortify the most indigest and crude stomach, ah, were it of one that through extreme weakness vomited blood, applying only a warm napkin to the place, after the unction and fricace; for the vertigine in the head, putting but a drop in your nostrils, likewise behind the ears; a most sovereign and approved remedy: the *mal caduco*, cramps, convulsions, paralyses, epilepsies, *tremor cordia*, retired nerves, ill vapours of the spleen, stopping of the liver, the stone, the strangury, *hernia ventosa*, *iliaca passio*; stops a *dysenteria* immediately; easeth the torsion of the small guts; and cures *melancholy hypocondriaca*, being taken and applied according to my printed receipt. For this is the physician, this the medicine; this counsels, this cures; this gives the direction, this works the effect; and, in sum, both together may be termed an abstract of the theoric and practic in the Aesculapian art...
>
> (*Volpone*, act 2, scene 2)

This passage, full of Latin terms, is not only a brilliantly written comic catalogue but it also a parody of the quack's artful pitch for medical remedies that cure everything from spitting blood to hernias. The passage can be seen, by extension, as a parody of quack medical advertising and, by extension, of advertising in general.

10. *Chase Scenes (visual)*

Chase scenes involve a character being chased, for one reason or another, by other characters (such as Buster Keaton being chased by thousands of policemen in *Cops*). The character being chased uses ingenuity and various comic ploys to escape being caught.

Keaton is not caught in *Cops;* after having been chased by an entire police force and eluding them, ironically, at the end of the film, having been spurned by the woman he loves, he turns himself in. Chase scenes aren't always humorous of course; they are a standard dramatic technique used in serious (as opposed to humorous) dramas like police adventures and thrillers.

11. *Coincidences (logic)*

As the result of chance, characters often find themselves in awkward, uncomfortable or embarrassing situations—which audiences find amusing. Coincidence is often paired with another technique, revelation and unmasking, in which characters who are pretending to be virtuous are exposed for their true nature, or men who are pretending to be women are discovered.

In Sheridan's *The School for Scandal*, there is a scene in which Joseph Surface, a man who pretends to be virtuous but is really a scoundrel, has lured Lady Teazle, the attractive young wife of Sir Peter Teazle, his potential benefactor, to his apartment. He intends to seduce her. Joseph is explaining that Lady Teazle suffers from too much virtue and that she should sin to preserve her reputation.

JOSEPH:	Then, by this hand, which he is unworthy of— [*Taking her hand*] *Re-enter* SERVANT 'Sdeath, you blockhead—what do you want?
SERVANT:	I beg your pardon, sir, but I thought you would not choose Sir Peter to come up without announcing him.
JOSEPH:	Sir Peter!—Oons—the devil!

LADY TEAZLE:	Sir Peter! O Lud! I'm ruined! I'm ruined!
SERVANT:	T'wasn't I let him in.
LADY TEAZLE:	Oh! I'm quite undone! What will become of me? Now, Mr. Logic—Oh! mercy, sir, he's on the stairs—I'll get behind here—and if I'm ever so imprudent again—[*Goes behind the screen*]
JOSEPH:	Give me that book. [*Sits down.* SERVANT *pretends to adjust his chair.*] *Enter* SIR PETER TEAZLE
SIR PETER:	Ay, ever improving himself. Mr. Surface, Mr. Surface.

(*The School for Scandal*, act 4, scene 3)

Sir Peter's arrival interrupts Joseph Surface's attempt to seduce Sir Peter's wife and leads to a situation where she hides and can overhear the conversation between Joseph and her husband. Sir Peter comes to tell him that he thinks his wife has formed an attachment to someone else—namely Charles Surface.

JOSEPH:	"My brother! impossible!"
SIR PETER:	Oh, my dear friend, the goodness of your own heart misleads you. You judge of others by yourself.
JOSEPH:	Certainly, Sir Peter, the heart that is conscious of its own integrity is ever slow to credit another's treachery.

(*The School for Scandal*, act 4, scene 3)

We have an example here of ignorance or discrepant awareness, since Sir Peter does not know his wife is in the apartment, hidden behind a screen. A short while later, Joseph's servant announces that Joseph's brother, Charles, is coming to visit. Sir Peter instructs Joseph to quiz Charles about his relationship with Lady Teazle and hides in a closet.

So we have two people hiding in different parts of the apartment, with Sir Peter unaware that his wife is hiding behind the screen and Charles unaware that Sir Peter and Lady Teazle are there, hidden away. These chance visits, which I describe as coincidences, lead to the comic situation—one that will lead, eventually, to Joseph Surface being revealed as a hypocrite and scoundrel.

12. *Comparisons (logic)*

Analogies, mentioned earlier, involve comparisons, but they are indirect. They always involve metaphors or similes. Comparisons (as I use the term) are direct and use other techniques such as insult or ridicule to generate their humor.

In Sheridan's *The School for Scandal*, there is a bit of dialogue in which two brothers, Joseph Surface and Charles Surface, are compared. Joseph is a hypocrite and scoundrel, but has the reputation for being virtuous, and Charles is virtuous but has the reputation of being a scoundrel. In this bit of dialogue, one of the characters, Snake, is discussing the two brothers with Lady Sneerwell, a malicious gossip and scandal mongerer.

> SNAKE: But, Lady Sneerwell, there is one affair in which you have lately employed me, wherein, I confess, I am at a loss to guess your motives.
>
> SNEERWELL: I conceive you mean with respect to my neighbor, Sir Peter Teazle and his family.
>
> SNAKE: I do. Here are two young men, to whom Sir Peter has acted as a kind of guardian since their father's death; the eldest, possessing the most amiable character, and universally well spoken of—the youngest, the most dissipated and extravagant young fellow in the kingdom, without friends or character: the former an avowed admirer of your ladyship, and apparently your favourite; the latter attached to Maria, Sir Peter's ward, and confessedly beloved by her.
>
> (*The School For Scandal*, act 1, scene 1)

A short while later in their discussion, Lady Sneerwell reveals that Joseph Surface is a fraud and is really "artful, selfish, and malicious" who "passes for a youthful miracle of prudence, good sense, and benevolence." It turns out that she loves Charles and has formed an alliance with Joseph, who pretends to like Lady Sneerwell but really is after Maria for her money.

This dialogue is found in the opening scene of the play, and establishes the plot immediately: Joseph Surface is a fraud but most of the characters in the play do not know this. We have the matter of discrepant awareness established; will Joseph be able to fool everyone (except his confederates, that is) or will he somehow be unmasked? The comparison and the dialogue that follows establishes the central conflict in the play. We have a situation where Lady Sneerwell loves Charles Surface, who loves and is loved by Maria, who is desired (for her wealth) by Joseph Surface. Lady Sneerwell is helping Joseph Surface so she can get Charles, and Joseph can marry Maria.

13. *Definitions (language)*

Comic definitions are often used by humorists. Their definitions involve other techniques such as insult, sarcasm and ridicule. We also find humorous definitions amusing because they involve defeated expectations—we expect something serious (since we associate definitions with dictionaries) and get something frivolous.

In *Henry IV, Part I* there is a famous definition of the term "honor" by Falstaff, as he responds to a statement by Hal:

> PRINCE: Why, thou owest God a death. [Exit.]
>
> FALSTAFF: 'Tis not due yet: I would be loath to pay him before his day. What need I be so forward with him that calls not on me? Well, 'tis no matter: honor pricks me on. Yea, but how if honor prick me off when I come on? How then? Can honor set to a leg? No. Or an arm? No. Or take away the grief of a wound? No. Honor hath no skill at surgery then? No. What is honor? A word. What is that word honor? Air. A trim reckoning. Who hath it? He that died a Wednesday. Doth he feel it? No. Doth he hear it? No. 'Tis insensible then? Yea, to the dead. But will [it] not live with the living? No. Why? Detraction will not suffer it. Therefore I'll none of it. Honor is a mere scutcheon—and so ends my catechism. [Exit.]
>
> (*Henry IV, Part I*, act 5, scene 2)

This passage is not whimsical and full of laughs, though it does have some wordplay in it. It helps establish the character of Falstaff as a realist (and perhaps a coward). As such, it is connected to an element of humor that acknowledges what might be described as the profoundly absurd nature of life, in which people often, and sometimes foolishly, lay down their lives for mere "words."

We now move to a discussion of disappointments and defeated expectations—one of the more important techniques of humor, especially since it is often connected with sexual relationships.

14. *Disappointments and Defeated Expectations (logic)*

In this technique, a person's expectations (often of a sexual nature) are led on and then, at the last moment, denied as a result of an accident, coincidence, misunderstanding, or something of that nature. Humor involving sexual frustration is very common in American culture according to sociologists who have studied the matter.

One of the best examples in Shakespearean comedy of this technique is found in *The Merry Wives of Windsor*. Falstaff has written letters declaring his love to two women he finds attractive, Mrs. Ford and Mrs. Page. He tells a friend that Mrs. Ford has shown, by her actions, that she's attracted to him.

FALSTAFF: I have writ me here a letter to her: and here another to Page's wife; who even now gave me good eyes, too, examined my parts with most judicious eyeliads: sometimes the beam of her view gilded my food, sometimes my portly belly.

(*The Merry Wives of Windsor*, act 1, scene 3)

Mrs. Ford and Mrs. Page are good friends and after showing one another Falstaff's letters, which are identical, decide to teach him a lesson.

MRS. PAGE: Let's be revenged on him: let's appoint him a meeting: give him a show of comfort in his suit; and lead him on with a fine baited delay...

(*The Merry Wives of Windsor*, act 2, scene 1)

The situation becomes more complicated because Falstaff has met a person in an Inn (who is Mr. Ford in disguise) who carries on, in great detail, about how much he loves Mrs. Ford. Falstaff then says "you shall, if you will, enjoy Ford's wife." Next Falstaff boasts that he has arranged a tryst with Mrs. Ford.

FALSTAFF: I shall be with her between ten and eleven; for at that time the jealous rascally knave, her husband, will be forth.

(*The Merry Wives of Windsor*, act 2, scene 1)

Falstaff adds that he will use Mrs. Ford as the "key of the cuckoldly rogue's coffer," so there's more to his profession of love to Mrs. Ford than lust. All of this leads to the great scene in which Falstaff goes to Mrs. Ford's house for what he thinks is a tryst and declares his love for her. But before anything can happen he is told that Mr. Ford is coming and thus must hide in a laundry basket to escape detection. Falstaff experiences here "defeated expectations," one of the most important techniques used in comedies.

15. *Eccentricity (identity)*

Writers use characters who are eccentric and bizarre, one way or another, to create humor. These eccentrics usually represent certain types—misers, misanthropes, drunkards, liars, braggarts, poseurs—who cannot control themselves and usually end up outsmarting themselves and learning painful lessons.

In this respect, let us consider the hero of Samuel Beckett's *Krapp's Last Tape*. He reveals his eccentricity throughout the play, with his comments and his remarkable tapes, but there are several scenes of particular interest:

> KRAPP: Good to be back in my den, in my old rags. Have just eaten I regret to say three bananas and only with difficulty refrained from a fourth. Fatal things for a man with my condition.

Then, a short while later, we find the following bit of dialogue from Krapp that gives more insight into his personality:

> KRAPP: Statistics. Seventeen hundred hours, out of the preceding eight-thousand-odd, consumed on licensed premises alone. More than 20 percent, say 40 percent of his waking life. (*Pause*) Plans for a less (*hesitates*)...engrossing sexual life. Last illness of his father. Flagging pursuit of unattainable laxation. Sneers at what he calls his youth and thanks to God that it's over.

In this brief play, Beckett uses a telegraphic style to create his remarkable character, who, we must remember, is shown with a white face and a purple nose, suggesting to the audience that he is some kind of clown figure.

16. *Embarrassment and Escape from It (identity)*

Characters who find themselves in situations in which they are made to feel uncomfortable, shamed, self-conscious or ridiculous, are embarrassed, as I use the term. They inevitably seek to escape from these situations and the events that lead to their embarrassments. Comedies frequently involve characters who get into messes and then do all kinds of things to get out of them, so the technique of embarrassment is of central importance.

There's a classic scene in Shakespeare's *The Merry Wives of Windsor* in which Falstaff thinks he has arranged a tryst with a married woman, Mrs. Ford. Falstaff has said to a friend earlier that he plans to make love to her.

> FALSTAFF: Briefly, I do mean to make love to Ford's wife; I spy entertainment in her; she discourses, she carves, she gives leer of invitation.
> (*The Merry Wives of Windsor*, act 1, scene 2)

Actually, he has been set up by Mrs. Ford and her friend, Mrs. Page, who want to teach him a lesson. Just after Falstaff declares his love for

Mrs. Ford, Mrs. Page runs in and informs Mrs. Ford that her husband is returning home, unexpectedly, to search the house.

> MRS. PAGE: Look, here is a basket; if he be of any reasonable stature, he may creep in here; and throw foul linen on him, as if were going to bucking: or, is it whiting-time, send him by your two men to Datchet Mead.
>
> (*The Merry Wives of Windsor*, act 3, scene 3)

Falstaff creeps into the basket and thus thinks he has avoided being caught by Mr. Ford. Mrs. Ford's men carry him away in the basket full of dirty linen and dump him into the Thames. In actuality, Falstaff has been the victim of a practical joke. He's an old lecher and is made to "pay," by being dumped in the Thames, for his continual and foolish attempts to seduce women.

17. *Exaggeration (language)*

By exaggeration I mean enhancing reality and blowing things up far beyond the reality of the situation. Exaggeration is the technique found in "tall tales." Exaggeration can also be reversed, leading to humorous understatement.

Sometimes the exaggeration is direct, as in a description a person makes of some event or object; at other times, it is indirect, and we can see the person exaggerating. Thus, in the wonderful scene in *Henry IV, Part I,* as Falstaff is describing a fight he was allegedly involved in, the number of people he says he fought with keeps growing: Prince Hal was actually there and thus actually knows what happened.

We find the following dialogue:

> PRINCE: Pray God you have not murdered some of them.
>
> FALSTAFF: Nay, that's past praying for. I have peppered two of them. Two I am sure I have paid, two rogues in buckram suits. I tell thee what, Hal, if I tell thee a lie, spit in my face, call me horse. Thou knowest my old ward. Here I lay, and thus I bore my boint. Four rogues in buckram let drive at me.
>
> PRINCE: What, four? Thou saidst but two even now.
>
> FALSTAFF: Four, Hal. I told thee four.
>
> POINS: Ay, ay, he said four.
>
> FALSTAFF: These four came all affront and mainly thrust at me. I made me no more ado but took all their seven points in my target, thus.

Comic Techniques in Dramatic Comedies   19

PRINCE: Seven? Why there were but four even now.
FALSTAFF: In buckram?
POINS: Ay, four in buckram suits.
FALSTAFF: Seven, by these hilts, or I am a villain else.
PRINCE: (*aside* to POINS) Prithee, let him alone. We shall have more anon.
FALSTAFF: Dos't thou hear me, Hal?
PRINCE: Ay, and mark thee too, Jack.
FALSTAFF: Do so, for it is worth listening to. These nine in buckram that I told thee of—
PRINCE: So, two more already.
FALSTAFF: Their points being broken—
POINTS: Down fell their hose.
FALSTAFF: Began to give me ground; but I followed me close, came in, foot and hand, and with a thought, seven of the eleven I paid.

(*Henry IV, Part I*, act 2, scene 4)

Thus, in the course of a short bit of dialogue, Falstaff raises the number of men who attacked him from two to eleven—revealing that he not only is a fabricator, but that playing loose with the truth and exaggerating things is so much a part of his personality that he doesn't even recognize what he is doing. Falstaff is, of course, one of the greatest comic creations in dramatic literature.

18. *Exposure (identity)*

In exposure, characters inadvertently reveal something about themselves—often of a sexual nature—or sometimes, as the result of a mistake or coincidence, expose their bodies (they are shown naked or partly naked). We are generally amused when people who try to hide aspects of their sexual lives or who try to prevent their bodies from being seen are unsuccessful in doing so. At other times, characters are exposed as frauds, liars, cowards, impersonators, and so on.

We find revelation of character in the scene described above, where Falstaff is shown exaggerating with wild abandon. Just after Falstaff has exaggerated the number of men he has killed, the Prince calls Falstaff's bluff:

PRINCE: We two saw you four set on four, and bound them and were masters of their wealth. Mark now, how a plain tale shall put you down. Then

	did we two set on your four, and with a word, outfaced you from your prize, and have it; yea, and can show it you here in the house. And, Falstaff, you carried your guts away as nimbly, with as quick dexterity, and roared for mercy, and still run and roared, as ever I heard bullcalf. What a slave art thou to hack thy sword as thou hast done, and then say it was in fight! What trick, what device, what starting hole can'st thou now find out to hide thee from this open and apparent shame?
POINS:	Come, let's hear Jack. What trick hast thou now?

(Henry IV, Part 1, act 2, scene 4)

Falstaff is thus exposed as a comic fraud, and in a play frame, exposing people who pretend to be what they are not or exposing people who are impersonating others is a source of humor. There is an element of comic tension generated involving exposure: will fakes be discovered? Much of the humor here involves discrepant awareness: a discrepancy between what some characters know and what others don't know or what the audience knows and what other characters don't know. A good deal of humor, as we shall see in my analyses of some classic plays, involves people pretending to be someone else or pretending to be different from the way they really are.

Another commonly used comic technique involves escape from embarrassment, and that is what we find in Falstaff's answer to Prince Hal:

FALSTAFF:	By the Lord, I knew ye as well as he that made ye. Why, hear you, my masters: Was it for me to kill the heir apparent? Should I turn upon the true prince? Why, thou knowest I am as valiant as Hercules, but beware instinct. The lion will not touch the true prince. Instinct is a great matter.

Falstaff is a trickster figure, who continually escapes, one way or another, from embarrassments, from traps that others set for him or from difficult situations he gets himself into.

19. *Facetiousness (language)*

Facetiousness refers to a joking, frivolous, nonserious use of language and attitude by a character. The problem with being facetious is that one can easily be misunderstood; somehow the fact that one is being facetious must be made clear to one's audience.

We see an excellent example of facetiousness in Falstaff's description of himself and his colleagues not as robbers but as "Diana's foresters." He is talking to Prince Hal:

FALSTAFF: Marry, then, sweet wag, when thou art king let not us that are squires of the night's body be called thieves of the day's beauty. Let us be Diana's foresters, gentlemen of the shade, minions of the moon; and let men say we be men of good government, being governed as the sea is, by our noble and chaste mistress the moon, under whose countenance we steal.

(*Henry IV, Part I*, act 1, scene 2)

Here Falstaff is being facetious and using language playfully to describe thieving as being one of Diana's foresters and thieves as being "minions of the moon."

20. *Grotesque (identity)*

A grotesque is a character who pushes the matter of eccentricity to almost painful ends. The grotesque isn't always comic, but if the grotesques are not physically deformed or terribly ugly and have elements about them such as absurdity, single-mindedness and eccentricity, we see grotesques as comic. We can also use the term to apply to types of characters and situations.

Thus, for example, a character like Volpone, who lives only for gold, can be seen as a grotesque. And so are the other characters in the play, the dupes who hope to inherit his wealth when he dies. Certain types of characters who are monomaniacs, who have zany rigidities—misers, misanthropes, pedants, and so on, are generally seen as comic grotesques.

21. *Ignorance, Gullibility, Naïveté (logic)*

Ignorant characters who are gulls, fools, or stupid are found in many comedies. We find the revelation of ignorance by characters amusing (perhaps because we feel "superior" to these ignorant characters). We also find the "creation of ignorance" in a character who is deceived by other characters, such as an impersonator, amusing. There are, I would suggest, two kinds of comic ignorance: some characters are stupid and reveal their ignorance in the course of the play, while others are "made" ignorant by other characters' trickery and deception.

This latter kind of ignorance has been termed "discrepant awareness" and is a major element in comedies. In some cases, members of the audience know things that some characters don't know (that a certain character is a male pretending to be a woman, for example). In other cases, the audience itself is made to experience "discrepant awareness" and doesn't know what one (or more) of the characters in the play knows.

Thus in *Twelfth Night* Malvolio, Olivia's steward, doesn't know that a letter he finds was not written by Olivia but by her maid, Maria, and is a forgery, part of a practical joke being played on him. And he does not know, when he is prancing in Olivia's garden and talking to himself, that he is being overheard by Maria, Sir Toby Belch, Sir Andrew Aguecheek (two comic characters in their own right) and a servant, Fabian. They comment, to the audience, on Malvolio's statements.

MALVOLIO: 'Tis but fortune, all is fortune. Maria once told me she did affect me. And I have heard herself come thus near, that, should she fancy, it should be one of my complexion. Besides, she uses me with a more exalted respect than anyone else that follows her. What should I think on 't?

SIR TOBY: Here's an overweening rogue!

FABIAN: Oh, peace! Contemplation makes a rare turkeycock of him. How he jets under his advanced plumes!

SIR ANDREW: 'Slight, I could so beat the rogue!

SIR TOBY: Peace, I say.

MALVOLIO: To be Count Malvolio.

SIR TOBY: Ah, rogue!

SIR ANDREW: Pistol him, pistol him.

SIR TOBY: Peace, peace!

MALVOLIO: There is an example for 't. The lady of Strachy married the yeoman of the wardrobe.

SIR ANDREW: Fie on him, Jezebel!

FABIAN: Oh, peace! Now he's deeply in. Look how imagination blows him.

MALVOLIO: Having been three months married to her, sitting in my state—

SIR TOBY: Oh, for a stonebow, to hit him in the eye!

MALVOLIO: Calling my officers about me, in my branched velvet gown, having come from a day bed, where I have left Olivia sleeping—

SIR TOBY: Fire and brimstone!

FABIAN: Oh, peace, peace!

MALVOLIO: And then to have the humor of state. And after a demure travel of regard, telling them I know my place as I would they should do theirs, to ask for my kinsman Toby—

SIR TOBY: Bolts and shackles!

FABIAN: Oh, peace, peace, peace! Now, now.

MALVOLIO:	Seven of my people, with an obedient start, make out for him. I frown the while, and perchance wind up my watch, or play with my—some rich jewel. Toby approaches, curtsies there to me—
SIR TOBY:	Shall this fellow live?
FABIAN:	Though our silence be drawn from us with cars, yet peace.
MALVOLIO:	I extend my hand to him thus, quenching my familiar smile with an austere regard of control—
SIR ANDREW:	And does not Toby take you a blow o' the lips then?
MALVOLIO:	Saying, "Cousin Toby, my fortunes having cast me on your niece, give me this prerogative of speech—
SIR TOBY:	What, what?
MALVOLIO:	"You must amend your drunkenness."
SIR TOBY:	Out, scab!
FABIAN:	Nay, patience, or we break the sinews of our plot.
MALVOLIO:	"Besides, you waste the treasure of your time with a foolish knight—"
SIR ANDREW:	That's me, I warrant you.
MALVOLIO:	"One Sir Andrew—"

(*Twelfth Night*, act 2, scene 5)

This scene is a classic example of ignorance or discrepant awareness. It is one in which people who are being talked about are hidden and overhear what is being said about them, while the speaker is unaware that this is the case. Often, in such situations, the speaker says insulting things about those who are hidden. Thus, the speaker ridicules those who are hiding, but the speaker is also being ridiculed for not knowing his or her words are being overheard. I discuss this matter in more detail in my chapter on *Twelfth Night* in the second section of this book.

22. *Imitation and Pretense (identity)*

Imitation, as I use the term, involves a character pretending to be something else—a dog, a chair, a robot (as in Woody Allen's *Sleepers*)—or in a different state (a dying man, as in *Volpone*).

In *Volpone*, at the end of act 1, scene 2, Volpone describes the situation, as Mosca exits, to bring in Voltore:

VOLPONE:	Now, my feigned cough, my phthysis, and my gout, My apoplexy, palsy, and catarrhs, Help, with your forced functions, this my posture, Wherein, this three years, I have milked their hopes. He comes, I hear him—uh! uh! uh! uh! O—

When Voltore enters, Volpone imitates a dying man:

VOLPONE: I feel me going, uh! uh! uh! uh!
I am sailing to my port, uh! uh! uh! uh!

Mosca tells Voltore that he will inherit everything of Volpone's—which is what Mosca tells all of the people who bring Volpone gifts—hoping to get on his good side and inherit all his wealth.

23. *Impersonation (identity)*

I differentiate between imitation and impersonation. Imitation, as I have just suggested, involves a character pretending to be something else. Impersonation involves a character taking on someone else's identity or a profession (such as a doctor). The impersonator often "degrades" the character being impersonated (or the profession). There is always a tension created—will the impersonator be discovered? There is also the question as to what mischief the impersonator will accomplish.

In *Twelfth Night*, after Malvolio has been locked up because he is thought to be mad, the clown puts on a gown and pretends to be Sir Topas, the curate.

[Enter MARIA and CLOWN.]

MARIA: Nay, I prithee put on this gown and this beard. Make him believe thou art Sir Topas the curate. Do it quickly. I'll call Sir Toby the whilst. [exit.]

CLOWN: Well, I'll put it on, and I will dissemble myself in 't, and I would I were the first that ever dissembled in such a gown.

(*Twelfth Night*, act 4, scene 2)

A short while later the Clown, dressed as Sir Topas, visits Malvolio, who is in a dark dungeon. This leads to a conversation between Malvolio and the Clown, who is impersonating Sir Topas.

MALVOLIO: [*Within*] Who calls there?
CLOWN: Sir Topas the curate, who comes to visit Malvolio the lunatic.
MALVOLIO: Sir Topas, Sir Topas, good Sir Topas, go to my lady.
CLOWN: Out, hyperbolical fiend! How vexst thou this man! Talkest thou nothing but of ladies?

(*Twelfth Night*, act 4, scene 2)

The conversation continues, with Malvolio unaware that he's been fooled, another example of ignorance and discrepant awareness.

Impersonation must involve some kind of ignorance on the part of some characters, who, for example, when they are attracted to men pretending to be women, make fools of themselves. Of course in comedies, characters are always making fools of themselves—one way or another.

24. *Infantilism (language)*

Infantilism, as I interpret the term, involves an adult character using the language of a baby and playing around with words, uttering nonsense terms and that kind of thing. Let me offer several brief examples. In Tom Stoppard's *Travesties* there is a scene in which Carr and Tristan Tzara are discussing art.

CARR:	It is the duty of the artist to beautify existence.
TZARA:	(*articulately*): Dada dada dada dada dada dada dada dada dada dada dada dada dada dada dada dada dada dada dada dada dada dada dada dada dada dada dada dada dada dada dada dada dada dada.
CARR:	(*slight pause*) Oh, what nonsense you talk!
TZARA:	It may be nonsense, but at least it's not clever nonsense. Cleverness has been exploded, along with so much else, by the war.

(*Travesties*, act 1)

I see this as infantilism rather than absurdity because the term "dada" is found in infancy and we are not dealing with the perversion of logic, which we find in absurdity. We also find infantilism in *The Bald Soprano*, used by Ionesco to attack rationality and logic. At the end of the play, we find Mrs. Smith doing the same thing Tzara did, repeating a word over and over again. Mr. and Mrs. Smith are having a conversation with their guests, the Martins.

MR. MARTIN:	I'd rather kill a rabbit than sing in the garden.
MRS. SMITH:	Cockatoos, cockatoos, cockatoos, cockatoos, cockatoos, cockatoos, cockatoos, cockatoos, cockatoos, cockatoos, cockatoos.
MRS. SMITH:	Such caca, such caca, such caca, such caca, such caca, such caca, such caca, such caca, such caca.
MR. MARTIN:	Such cascades of cacas, such cascades of cacas, such cascades of cacas, such cascades of cacas, such cascades of cacas, such cascades of cacas, such cascades of cacas, such cascades of cacas.

MR. SMITH: Dogs have fleas, dogs have fleas.
MRS. MARTIN: Cactus, coccyx! crocus! cockades! cockroach!

This dialogue also uses repetition and pattern and is similar to the language of infants as they learn how to play around with sounds, often making nonsensical sounds in the process. Caca is a comic (and one used by children at times) reference to defecation, which adds support to my notion that we have infantile soundplay and wordplay here. In this case we have infantilism and nonsense; we have the use of infantile sound play, added to repetition and pattern, to generate absurdity and nonsense.

25. *Insults (language)*

A humorous insult is the direct use of verbal aggression to degrade a person or some other object (such as an institution) for comic effect. Insults often involve wild comparisons, attacks on sexual aspects of a person, allusions to embarrassing things done in the past and that kind of thing. Insults are not humorous in themselves, so they must use other techniques to create the humor and the insulter must make certain that the insults are not seen as "real," but are tied to a role in a play or as part of one's act or something like that. (That is, there must be a play frame.) Insults are very dangerous ways to generate laughter, but are commonly used. Insults that are reversed and directed at oneself yield "victim" humor.

In *Travesties* Stoppard makes good use of comic insults in a number of places. In one scene, Carr, the central character of the play, insults Tzara:

CARR: My God, you little Rumanian wog—you bloody dago—you jumped-up phrase-making smart-alecy arty-intellectual Balkan turd!!! Think you know it all!—while we poor dupes think we're fighting for ideals, you've got a profound understanding of what is *really* going on, underneath—you've got a phrase for it! You pedant!

(*Travesties*, act 1)

Later in the act, we have James Joyce and Tristan Tzara insulting each other:

TZARA: By God, you supercilious streak of Irish puke! You four-eyed, bog-ignorant, potato-eating ponce! Your art has failed. You've turned literature into a religion and it's as dead as all the rest, it's an overripe corpse and you're cutting fancy figures at the wake....

(*Travesties*, act 1)

Joyce then replies, in a much milder manner, as follows:

> JOYCE: You are an over-excited little man, with a need for self-expression far beyond the scope of your natural gifts. This is not discreditable. Neither does it make you an artist...
>
> (*Travesties*, act 1)

Stoppard is using comic insult here to delineate his characters better and to discuss the nature of art. Comic insults are found in many humorous texts, sometimes directed at particular individuals with whom one is conversing. At other times they are directed at characters in a play who are not on stage when the insults are made (but who may be overhearing them). At other times, insults are directed at institutions, kinds of people (parents, children, mothers-in-law), occupations (psychiatrists, professors, priests, rock stars, etc.), nationalities, religions, and so on.

26. *Irony (language)*

Eirons, characters who are wise and pretend to be dumb, or powerful and pretend to be weak, or deceitful but pretend to be honest, are stock figures in comedy. Irony is a very complicated subject. Verbal irony involves saying one thing but meaning the opposite (and trying to make sure that your real meaning is understood). Dramatic irony refers to situations in plots: a character pursues some goal but gets the opposite of what he or she seeks.

Volpone is a masterpiece full of both verbal and dramatic irony. Volpone, who has duped a number of people trying to get him to leave them his fortune, is duped in the end by his servant Mosca. Rather than allow Mosca to steal all his money, Volpone confesses to what he has been doing and is sent to a hospital where he is to be put in chains and left to suffer the ills he claimed to have suffered from. In one bitterly ironic scene, Volpone and Mosca are talking.

> MOSCA: Alas, sir, I but do as I am taught;
> Follow your grave instructions; give 'em words;
> Pour oil into their ears, and send them hence.
>
> VOLPONE: 'Tis true, 'tis true. What a rare punishment is avarice to itself.
>
> (*Volpone*, act 1, scene 4)

Volpone (wolf) here is talking about Voltore (vulture), Corbaccio (raven), and Corvino (crow), but he will discover, eventually, that the words he utters—that avarice is a punishment—apply to him more than others.

There is another classic scene at the beginning of the play when Mosca is talking to Volpone about the way he lives, which is a wonderful example of irony.

> MOSCA: And, besides, sir,
> You are not like the thresher that doth stand
> With a huge flail, watching a heap of corn,
> And, hungry, dares not taste the smallest grain,
> But feeds on mallows and such bitter herbs;
> Nor like the merchant, who hath filled his vaults
> With Romagnia and rich Candian wines,
> Yet drinks the lees of Lombard's vinegar.
> You will not lie in straw, whilst moths and worms
> Feed on your sumptuous hangings and soft beds.
> You know the use of riches, and dare give, now,
> From that bright heap, to me, your poor observer,
> Or to your dwarf, or your hermaphrodite,
> Your eunuch, or what other household trifle
> Your pleasure allows maintenance—
>
> (*Volpone*, act 1, scene 1)

In truth, this description fits Volpone, who is very wealthy but gets no pleasure from his wealth and, most decidedly, does not know the use of riches. Mosca's tone is ironic, but Volpone does not recognize the irony and eventually, as punishment for his activities, will lie in straw.

27. *Literalness (language)*

Literalness, or more correctly, over-literalness, is the basis of moron jokes and much comedy. It involves characters who are stupid and take everything literally or who lack imagination and good sense—who are not flexible and who do not take circumstances into account. As Bergson wrote, "a comic effect is obtained whenever we pretend to take literally an expression which was used figuratively."

In *Twelfth Night* there is a great deal of wordplay and wit as well as the use of literalness. In act 3, scene 1, Viola and Feste, Olivia's clown, have a conversation in which literalness is used to generate humor. Viola, in this scene, is dressed as a male and is pretending to be a young man, Cesario.

[*Enter* VIOLA, *and* CLOWN *with a tabor.*]

VIOLA: Save thee, friend, and thy music. Dost thou live by thy tabor?

CLOWN: No, sir, I live by the church.

VIOLA: Art thou a churchman?

CLOWN: No such matter, sir. I do live by the church for I do live at my house, and my house doth stand by the church.

VIOLA: So thou mayst say the King lies by a beggar, if a beggar do dwell near him, or the church stands by thy tabor, if thy tabor stand by the church.

CLOWN: You have said, sir. To see this age! A sentence is but a chevril [kidskin] glove to a good wit. How quickly the wrong side may be turned outward!

VIOLA: Nay, that's certain. They that dally nicely with words may quickly make them wanton.

CLOWN: I would, therefore, my sister had no name, sir.

VIOLA: Why, man?

CLOWN: Why, sir, her name's a word, and to dally with that word might make my sister wanton. But indeed words are very rascals since bonds disgraced them.

VIOLA: Thy reason man?

CLOWN: Troth, sir, I can yield you none without words, and words are grown so false I am loath to prove reason with them.

At the beginning of this marvelous passage, we see the Clown taking the term "live by" literally, to toy with Viola. She says "live by" but means "occupation"—which he takes literally to mean "live near." Shortly after this conversation, the Clown describes himself not as Olivia's fool "but her corrupter of words." By this he means his job is to play around with words and their meanings. The problem is that words have "grown so false" that he can't use them with any hope that they will be interpreted correctly and can't use them to show people the truth. How does one reveal the truth or reason with people when the words one uses have become "false"? Playing with words and meanings, I might point out, is also one of the tasks of the writer of comedies and humor of all kinds.

28. *Mimicry (identity)*

In mimicry, a person maintains his own identity but imitates the voice and language of some famous individual such as Jimmy Stewart, John Wayne, Richard Nixon and so on. The mimic also uses other techniques to generate humor: body language, facial expressions, allusions to embarrassing events, ridicule, the revelation of ignorance, insults, and that kind of thing.

Shakespeare uses this technique in *Henry IV, Part I* when Henry, the Prince of Wales, mimics both Hotspur and his wife:

> PRINCE: I am not yet of Percy's mind, the Hotspur of the North, he that kills me some six or seven dozen of Scots at a breakfast, washes his hands, and says to his wife, "Fie upon this quiet life! I want work." "Oh my sweet Harry," says she, "how many hast thou killed to-day?" "Give my roan horse a drench," says he, and answers, "Some fourteen," an hour after; "a trifle, a trifle."
>
> (*Henry IV, Part I*, act 2, scene 4)

Harry does this by exaggerating Hotspur's exploits and imitating the way his wife speaks to him.

29. *Mistakes (logic)*

A mistake involves something one does, an error based on such things as poor judgment, inattention, inadequate information, or stupidity. Mistakes are one of the fundamental techniques found in comedy, which involves various kinds of stupid and silly errors. I differentiate between mistakes and misunderstandings, which are verbal in nature.

At one point in the play *Travesties,* there is a situation in which folders with written material by Lenin and Joyce are mistakenly switched. At the end of the play, this mistake is discovered:

> TZARA: (*handing* JOYCE *his folder*): Furthermore, your book has much in common with your dress. As an arrangement of words it is graceless without being random; as a narrative it lacks charm or even vulgarity; as an experience it is like sharing a cell with a fanatic in search of a mania.
> (GWEN *and* CECILY *enter.* JOYCE *is scanning the manuscript.*)
>
> JOYCE: Who gave you this manuscript to read?
>
> GWEN: I did!
>
> JOYCE: Miss Carr, did I or did I not give you to type a chapter in which Mr. Bloom's adventures correspond to the Homeric episode of the Oxen of the Sun?
>
> GWEN: Yes, you did! And it was wonderful!
>
> JOYCE: Then why do you return to me an ill-tempered thesis purporting to prove, amongst other things, that Ramsay MacDonald is a bourgeois lickspittle gentleman's gentleman?
>
> GWEN: (Aaaah)
>
> TZARA: (Ohhhh)

CECILY: (Oops!)
CARR: (Aaaah!)
JOYCE: (*thunders*): Miss Carr, where is the missing chapter???
CARR: Excuse me—did you say Bloom?
JOYCE: I did.
CARR: And is it a chapter, inordinate in length and erratic in style, remotely connected with midwifery?
JOYCE: It is a chapter which by a miracle of compression, uses the gamut of English literature from Chaucer to Carlyle to describe events taking place in a lying-in hospital in Dublin.
CARR: (*holding out his folder*): It is obviously the same work. (GWEN *and* CECILY *swap folders with cries of recognition.*)

(*Travesties*, act 2)

Notice that Stoppard also uses another technique here as well—insult. Carr says, in Joyce's presence, that his chapter is "inordinate in length and erratic in style," and Ramsay MacDonald is also insulted by Lenin, who describes him as a "bourgeois lickspittle gentleman's gentleman."

Describing this mistake doesn't do justice to the impact of the dialogue; in this scene the mistake and insults that follow are very funny.

30. *Misunderstanding (language)*

As I suggested above, mistakes are based on things people *do* while misunderstandings are, as I see things, primarily verbal in nature and involve characters not communicating effectively with one another. A misunderstanding is linguistic; nevertheless, it is still part of what might be described as the comedy of errors.

In *Twelfth Night* there is a classic scene that offers us a good example of a mistake that leads to a big misunderstanding. Malvolio has found a letter in which Olivia's handwriting has been forged by her maid, Maria. This letter contains lines that suggest to Malvolio that Olivia really loves him:

> I may command where I adore
> But silence, like a Lucrece knife,
> With bloodless stroke my heart doth gore.
> M, O, A, I, doth sway my life.
>
> (*Twelfth Night*, act 2, scene 5)

A bit later in the letter we find:

If this fall into thy hand, revolve. In my stars I am above thee; but be not afraid of greatness. Some are born great, others achieve greatness, and some have greatness thrust upon 'em. Thy Fates open their hands...Remember who commended thy yellow stockings, and wished to see thee ever cross-gartered. I say, remember. Go to, thou art made, if thou desirest to be so. If not, let me see thee a steward still, the fellow of servants, and not worthy to touch Fortune's fingers. Farewell. She what would alter services with thee,

THE FORTUNATE UNHAPPY

(*Twelfth Night*, act 2, scene 5)

Malvolio assumes this letter is Olivia's declaration of love. Notice the word *alter* sounds very much like *altar*, where people are married. Thus the stage is set for a misunderstanding. Malvolio appears dressed in yellow stockings with his garters crossed.

The notion that Malvolio is crazy is put in Olivia's mind by Maria, who tells her that Malvolio is acting very strange and "is sure possessed."

OLIVIA: Why, what's the matter? Does he rave?

MARIA: No, madam, he does nothing but smile. Your ladyship were best to have some guard about you if he come, for sure the man is tainted in 's wits.

(*Twelfth Night*, act 4, scene 4)

Olivia sends for Malvolio, who refers to the letter, which, of course, she knows nothing about. After a bit of gibberish, Olivia is worried about him and thinks he is ill.

When she asks, "Wilt thou go to bed, Malvolio?" he misinterprets the statement because of the forged letter and thinks that his wildest fantasies are to come true—that Olivia wants him to go to bed with her.

OLIVIA: Wilt thou go to bed, Malvolio?
MALVOLIO: To bed! Aye, sweetheart, and I'll come to thee.
OLIVIA: God comfort thee! Why dost thou smile so and kiss thy hand so oft?
MARIA: How do you, Malvolio?
MALVOLIO: At your request! Yes, nightingales answer daws.
MARIA: Why appear you with this ridiculous boldness before my lady?
MALVOLIO: "Be not afraid of greatness." 'Twas well writ.
OLIVIA: What meanest thou by that, Malvolio?
MALVOLIO: "Some are born great—"
OLIVIA: Ha!
MALVOLIO: "Some achieve greatness—"

OLIVIA:	What sayest thou?
MALVOLIO:	"And some have greatness thrust upon them."
OLIVIA:	Heaven restore thee!

(Twelfth Night, act 3, scene 4)

Olivia decides Malvolio has got a case of midsummer madness and has him taken away. Here a mistake, Malvolio's thinking the letter he received was from Olivia, led to a misunderstanding.

31. *Parody (identity)*

Parody involves such matters as the humorous imitation of:

A. the style of an author or creative artist (Hemingway);
B. a genre (soap operas); or
C. a particular text (*The Seventh Seal*)

One problem with parody is that audiences must be familiar with the original text that is being parodied to fully enjoy the parody, though audiences who don't know the text being parodied often can enjoy the parody as a humorous work in itself. I often show my students *Der Dove*, which is a parody of Bergman's *The Seventh Seal* and *Wild Strawberries* but my students generally have not seen Bergman's films and thus cannot "get" the parody, though they enjoy *Der Dove* in its own right. In Greek comedies, such as *The Birds*, there is a great deal of parodying of texts that modern audiences do not recognize because we are not familiar with the texts or styles being parodied.

Stoppard uses parody in *Travesties* where he has a section of the play that features an interrogation of Tzara by Joyce. A portion of this passage follows:

JOYCE:	Are you the inventor of this sport or pastime?
TZARA:	I am not.
JOYCE:	What is the name of the inventor?
TZARA:	Arp.
JOYCE:	Is he your sworn enemy, pet aversion, bête noire, or otherwise persona non grata?
TZARA:	He is not.
JOYCE:	Is he your friend, comrade-in-arms, trusted confidant or otherwise pal, mate or crony?

TZARA:	He is.
JOYCE:	By what familiarity, indicating possession and amicability in equal parts, do you habitually refer to him?
TZARA:	My friend Arp.
JOYCE:	Alternating with what colloquialism redolent of virtue and longevity?
TZARA:	Good old Arp.

(*Travesties*, act 1)

This dialogue continues for a number of pages, as Joyce picks pieces of paper, each containing a word from Shakespeare's Eighteenth Sonnet, off his hair and clothes. Tzara had cut up the poem and put the pieces in what turned out to be Joyce's hat—when Joyce put his hat on, the paper scattered all over him. (This matter was discussed earlier under *accident humor*.) We can see that Stoppard is parodying interrogations, while also playing with words, using catalogues and other comedic techniques.

32. *Puns, Wordplay, and Other Amalgamations (language)*

Puns and wordplay involve the clever use of language to amuse and entertain. Puns are a specific form of wordplay that uses a word's sound to mean two different things. Wordplay involves wit—clever comments relative to some situation—that are made in a timely manner. You cannot miss a beat if the witty comment is to be effective.

We find puns and wordplay in many comedies; they are probably the most widely used techniques of linguistic humor. In Tom Stoppard's *Travesties,* there is an excellent example of wordplay. In this scene, the characters take joy just in mouthing words with wonderful sounds, though their dialogue also furthers the plot.

GWEN:	Do you know Mr. Tzara, the poet?
JOYCE:	By sight, and reputation; but I am a martyr to glaucoma and inflation. Recently as I was walking down the Bahnhofstrasse my eye was caught by a gallery showcase and I was made almost insensible with pain.
GWEN:	Mr. Joyce has written a poem about it. It is something you two have in common.
JOYCE:	Hardly. Mr. Tzara's disability is monocular, and, by rumour, affected, whereas I have certificates for conjunctivitis, iritis and synechia, and am something of an international eyesore.
GWEN:	I mean poetry. I was thinking of your poem "Bahnhofstrasse", beginning

	"The eyes that mock me sign the way Whereto I pass at eve of day, Grey way whose violet signals are The trysting and the twining star."
TZARA:	(*to* JOYCE): For your masterpiece I have great expectorations. (GWEN's *squeak,* "*Oh!*") For you I would eructate a monument. (*Oh!*) Art for art's sake—I defecate!
GWEN:	Delectate...

(Travesties, act 1)

At the end of this dialogue we see Stoppard playing around with the "ate" sound in the following words: expectorate (spit), eructate (belch), defecate (shit), and delectate (delight). He also uses medical terminology to good effect, earlier in the dialogue. Stoppard employs various forms of linguistic humor throughout the play, as his characters argue about art and politics and numerous other matters.

33. *Repartee (language)*

The term repartee, as I use it, involves a character responding to slights, put downs, and veiled insults in a witty or clever manner. Repartee can make use of wordplay, allusion, odious comparison or other techniques of humor, but it must be timed perfectly, without missing a beat after the original provocation.

Wit, in general, involves making clever comments at a moment's notice, but isn't necessarily negative or insulting. It isn't, like repartee, a response to a slight of some kind by someone. Repartee, thus, is different from wit though a good repartee should be witty.

34. *Repetition, Pattern (logic)*

Repetition involves the humor of iteration and the ability of characters to cope with situations that repeat themselves and, often, deal with characters who have monomaniacal characteristics. Running gags are a good example of repetition and pattern: Jack Benny milked his definition of himself as a "cheapskate" for many years. Comic strips repeat the same relationship (*Krazy Kat*, for example, with Krazy, Offissa Pupp, and Ignatz Mouse) for decades. We know, more or less, what the pattern is but we don't know how the characters will find some new way to deal with it.

In Tom Stoppard's *Travesties* there's a fine example of the use of repetition for comic effect. There's a scene in which Carr, the lead character, is chatting with his manservant Bennett, and certain lines are repeated over and over again. In the play, we see Carr as an old man in some scenes and a young man in others. When he is an old man, his memory jumps and so certain scenes—what Stoppard calls "time slips"—are started over and over again, when Carr asks Bennett "Is there anything of interest?"

Let me offer several examples:

CARR: Is there anything of interest?
BENETT: The *Neue Zuricher Zeitung* and the *Zuricher Post* announce, respectively, an important Allied and German victory, each side gaining ground after inflicting heavy casualties on the other with little loss to itself.

(*Travesties*, act 1)

They continue to converse when Carr "slips" once again and asks:

CARR: Is there anything of interest?
BENNETT: There is a revolution in Russia, sir.
CARR: Really? What sort of revolution?
BENETT: A social revolution, sir.
CARR: A *social* revolution? Unaccompanied women smoking at the Opera, that sort of thing?...
BENNETT: Not precisely that, sir. It is more in the nature of a revolution of classes contraposed by the fissiparous disequilibrium of Russian society.

(*Travesties*, act 1)

Stoppard uses the line "Is there anything of interest" and repeats this pattern a number of times in this scene; he uses it later in the play, as well. This repetition shows Carr's faulty memory trying to reconstruct the past, but it also allows Stoppard to employ other humorous techniques as well, such as sarcasm, misunderstanding and wordplay. It also is used to recount some history.

35. *Reversal (logic)*

Reversal and contradiction involve things turning out differently from the way characters expect them to turn out. In some cases, characters get even with those who have tormented them, and in other cases, characters outsmart themselves and get a bit of their own medicine. Generally reversal is a consequence of exposure and revelation, and involves irony on the level of plot and behavior—though it can also be seen in language and dialogue.

In Sheridan's *The School for Scandal*, Joseph Surface is revealed to be a villain and his plot to marry his brother's love, Maria, is foiled. He ends up with nothing. And Lady Teazle leaves the company of Lady Sneerwell's group of gossips and dissemblers. That is a good example of plot reversal, following exposure.

For an example of linguistic reversal, let us look at Wilde's *The Importance of Being Earnest*. Jack has proposed to his love Gwendolyn.

> GWENDOLYN: Ernest, we may never be married. From the expression on mamma's face, I fear we never shall. Few parents nowadays pay any regard to what their children say to them. The old-fashioned respect for the young is fast dying out...
>
> (*The Importance of Being Earnest*, act 1)

I see this as reversal rather than irony, which is an indirect or implied form of reversal. In irony, you mean the opposite of what you say; in reversal, you twist conventional logic and speech. Thus, conventionally we say children don't pay regard to what their parents tell them and the old-fashioned respect by the young for the old is dying out; by reversing things, Wilde makes a humorous comment on society and its values.

Wilde does this same thing in another place, where Cecily is talking with Algernon, whom she has just met.

> ALGERNON: [*Raising his hat*] You are my little cousin Cecily, I'm sure.
>
> CECILY: You are under some strange mistake. I am not little. In fact, I believe I am more than usually tall for my age. [ALGERNON *is rather taken aback.*] But I am your cousin Cecily. You, I see from your card, are Uncle Jack's brother, my cousin Ernest, my wicked cousin Ernest.
>
> ALGERNON: Oh! I am not really wicked at all, cousin Cecily. You mustn't think that I am wicked.
>
> CECILY: If you are not, then you have been deceiving us all in a very inexcusable manner. I hope you have not been leading a double life, pretending to be wicked and being really good all the time. That would be hypocrisy.
>
> (*The Importance of Being Earnest*, act 2)

We can see that Wilde uses reversal to good effect, shocking people by taking conventional wisdom and turning it upside down, so to speak.

36. *Ridicule (language)*

Ridicule involves "making fun" and casting contemptuous laughter at someone or something. That is, we make individuals or institutions (or whatever) seem "ridiculous"—what Aristotle argued is the basis of comedy.

In *The Importance of Being Earnest*, Wilde ridicules the image of the young gentry as being idle and ignorant. We find this in a conversation between Jack and Lady Bracknell:

BRACKNELL: Do you smoke?

JACK: Well, yes, I must admit I smoke.

BRACKNELL: I am glad to hear it. A man should always have an occupation of some kind. There are far too many idle men in London as it is. How old are you?

JACK: Twenty-nine.

BRACKNELL: A very good age to be married at. I have always been of the opinion that a man who desires to get married should know either everything or nothing. Which do you know?

JACK: [*After some hesitation.*] I know nothing, Lady Bracknell.

BRACKNELL: I am pleased to hear it. I do not approve of anything that tampers with natural ignorance. Ignorance is like a delicate exotic fruit; touch it and the bloom is gone. The whole theory of modern education is radically unsound. Fortunately in England, at any rate, education produces no effect whatsoever. If it did, it would prove a serious danger to the upper classes, and probably lead to acts of violence in Grosvenor Square.

(*The Importance of Being Earnest*, act 1)

Wilde, through Lady Bracknell, is gently ridiculing English society and the supposedly idle wealthy classes.

37. *Rigidity (logic)*

I use the term rigidity to characterize people who are undeviating in their performance of certain kinds of behavior, who are unbending and dominated by an idée fixe or ruling passion. Bergson argued that the basis of comedy involves "the mechanical encrusted on the living" and it is rigidity that may be seen as another term for mechanical.

38. *Sarcasm (language)*

Sarcasm means "tearing the flesh" or "biting the lips in rage" and refers to the use of language that is contemptuous, mocking and wounding. Sarcastic remarks are obliquely, not directly, insulting—remarks that, by their *tone*, taunt and ridicule. They are bitter, cutting, caustic remarks that are extremely hostile.

We find an excellent example of sarcasm in Shakespeare's *Much Ado About Nothing*. In this play, two characters—Beatrice and Benedick loathe each other and continually make nasty remarks to one another. Hearing that he has come back from a battle, Beatrice asks a messenger:

> BEATRICE: I pray you, how many hath he killed and eaten in these wars? But how many hath he killed? for indeed, I promised to eat all of his killing.

When the messenger replies that Benedick is a good soldier, Beatrice continues with her sarcastic comments:

> BEATRICE: And a good soldier to a lady: but what is he to a lord?

Her uncle, Leonato, Governor of Messina, explains the relationship that exists between Beatrice and Benedick to the messenger.

> LEONATO: There is a kind of merry war betwixt Signior Benedick and her: they never meet but there is a skirmish of wit between them.

When they do meet they immediately start making sarcastic comments to one another.

> BEATRICE: I wonder that you will still be talking, Signior Benedick; nobody marks you.
> BENEDICK: What, my dear lady Disdain! are you yet living?
> BEATRICE: Is it possible disdain should die while she hath such meet food to feed it as Signior Benedick? Courtesy itself must convert to disdain if you come in her presence.
>
> (*Much Ado About Nothing*, act 1, scene 1)

Insults are direct and sarcasm is indirect, but at times it becomes difficult to separate one from the other.

39. *Satire (language)*

Defining satire is a very difficult and controversial matter. For our purposes satire is a technique that involves deriding and ridiculing stupidity, vice, and folly in individuals, institutions, and society. There is often an implicit moral dimension to satire; by pointing out how foolish we generally are, it suggests that alternatives to the status quo should be considered.

Oscar Wilde's *The Importance of Being Earnest* is a witty and satirical play, that, as we have seen, ridicules the social conventions of its time. Wilde gave his characters wonderfully witty comments to make about life, love, society, and so on. In this play, which was written in 1895, Algernon Moncrieff, a wealthy young man-about-town is visited by his friend from the country, John (Jack) Worthing. Jack has invented a young brother, Ernest, who supposedly lives in London and is always getting into trouble, which requires Jack to go to London to help him. In London, Jack takes the name of his made-up brother and calls himself Ernest. Algernon has also invented a character, Bunberry, who lives in the country and is frequently ill. Algernon, it turns out, often has to go to the country (where his ward Cecily lives) to help Bunberry.

JACK: Who is coming to tea?

ALGERNON: Oh! merely Aunt Augusta and Gwendolyn.

JACK: How perfectly delightful!

ALGERNON: Yes, that is all very well; but I am afraid Aunt Augusta won't quite approve of your being here.

JACK: May I ask why?

ALGERNON: My dear fellow, the way you flirt with Gwendolyn is perfectly disgraceful. It is almost as bad as the way Gwendloyn flirts with you.

JACK: I am in love with Gwendolyn. I have come up to town expressly to propose to her.

ALGERNON: I thought you had come up for pleasure?...I call that business.

JACK: How utterly unromantic you are!

ALGERNON: I really don't see anything romantic in proposing. It is very romantic to be in love. But there is nothing romantic about a definite proposal. Why, one may be accepted. One usually is, I believe. Then the excitement is all over. The very essence of romance is uncertainty. If ever I get married, I'll certainly try to forget the fact.

(*The Importance of Being Earnest*, act 1)

Jack has told Gwendolyn that his name is Ernest, the name he uses when in London. And when he proposes to her, she accepts, saying she always knew she would fall in love with someone named Ernest.

GWENDOLYN: We live, as I hope you know, Mr. Worthing, in an age of ideals. The fact is constantly mentioned in the more expensive monthly magazines, and has reached the provincial pulpits, I am told; and my ideal has always been to love some one of the name of Ernest. There is something in that name that inspires absolute confidence. The moment Algernon first mentioned to me that he had a friend called Ernest, I knew I was destined to love you.

JACK: You really love me, Gwendolyn?
GWENDOLYN: Passionately!
JACK: Darling! You don't know how happy you've made me.
GWENDOLYN: My own Ernest!
JACK: But you don't really mean to say that you couldn't love me if my name wasn't Ernest?
GWENDOLYN: But your name is Ernest.

(*The Importance of Being Earnest*, act 1)

A few lines later Jack asks her if she could love him if he had a different name, such as Jack.

GWENDOLYN: Jack?...No, there is very little music in the name Jack, if any at all, indeed. It does not thrill. It produces absolutely no vibrations....I have known several Jacks, and they all, without exception, were more than usually plain. Besides, Jack is a notorious domesticity for John! And I pity any woman who is married to a man called John. She would probably never be allowed to know the entrancing pleasure of a single moment's solitude. The only really safe name is Ernest.

(*The Importance of Being Earnest*, act 1)

It turns out at the end of the play that Jack had been found in a handbag and that, ironically, his name actually was Ernest, so everything is resolved very nicely. We can see from the quality of this dialogue how clever and witty Wilde was.

The play is full of satirical epigrams such as "In matters of grave importance, style, not sincerity, is the vital thing" and "All women become like their mothers. That is their tragedy. No man does. That's his." Wilde is satirizing Victorian conventions and society in a flippant, witty and inventive play about two wealthy young men who are both, in a sense, impostors. Jack pretends to be someone else (his younger brother, Ernest) and Algernon invents a friend (a character, Bunberry, who he must visit from time to time in the country).

The Importance of Being Earnest plays an important role in Tom Stoppard's *Travesties* for it is the play that James Joyce produces and in which Henry Carr, the lead actor in the play, stars. The names of the women in *Travesties* are those of the women in *The Importance of Being Earnest*, Gwendolyn and Cecily. Thus, there is an intertextual relationship involved in *Travesties*, and those familiar with the Wilde play can recognizes passages and events adapted from it in *Travesties* that are missed by those who have not read or seen *The Importance of Being Earnest*.

40. *Scale (identity)*

Scale can be used to create humor by contrasting characters in size and involving them in ridiculous situations or using objects that are either much too large or too small for the purposes at hand.

41. *Slapstick (visual)*

Slapstick is a physical form of comedy that involves characters having pies thrown in their faces, getting hit by mops, collisions between characters, slips on banana peels or greasy surfaces, comic fights, the destruction of objects (cars being torn apart, houses dismantled, etc.) and other such activities. Slapstick is considered "crude" but it is a very common technique of comedy and, as practiced by artists such as Chaplin or Laurel and Hardy, often was hilarious.

42. *Speed (visual)*

If we speed up certain actions, such as the way characters run in chase scenes or the way characters speak, these behaviors take on a humorous dimension. The reverse also applies, in which actions are slowed down and made ridiculous.

43. *Stereotypes (identity)*

A stereotype is a commonly held view about the characteristics and typical behavior patterns of some group of people based on matters such as ethnicity, race, nationality and religion (Poles, Jews, WASPs, African-Americans, Russians). Stereotypes can be positive, negative, or mixed—but generally they are negative when used by humorists. In comedies we find many stereotyped figures because they

Comic Techniques in Dramatic Comedies   43

provide an instant "explanation" of motivation and because they lend themselves beautifully to ridicule, insult, exaggeration, and other techniques as well.

We find this technique employed in Trevor Griffiths's play *Comedians*, which is about an evening school course in comedy held in a secondary school in Manchester, England. The course is being taught by Eddie Waters, and in the first act, while having a conversation with the students, Waters offers a number of stereotypes in an effort to show his students something about this technique and the nature of comedy. Waters asks the students to say a tongue twister, rapidly, "the traitor distrusts the truth." The students say the phrase in turn, ending with one of the students, Price.

PRICE: ....the traitor distrusts truth.

WATERS: *(finally, mild, matter-of-fact):* I've never liked the Irish, you know. Dr. Johnson said they were a very truthful race, they never spoke well of each other, but then how could they have? *(They look around, faintly puzzled, amused.)* Big, thick, stupid heads, large cabbage ears, hairy nostrils, daft eyes, fat, flapping hands, stinking of soil and Guinness. The niggers of Europe. Huge, uncontrollable wangers, spawning their degenerate kind wherever they're allowed to settle. I'd stop them settling here if I had my way. Send 'em back to the primordial bog they came from. Potato heads.
(Pause. MCBRAIN *clenches and unclenches his fists on the desk, watches them carefully.)*

CONNOR: *(slowly):* Would that be Southern Irish or Northern Irish, Mr. Waters?

WATERS: *(mildly on):* Or Jews, for that matter.

SAMUELS: What you staring at me for?
(Uneasy laughter, dying fast)

WATERS: *(still very matter-of-fact):* They have this *greasy* quality, do Jews. Stick to their own. Grafters. Fixers. Money. Always money. Say Jew, say gold. Moneylenders, pawn-brokers, usurers. They have the nose for it, you might say. Hitler put it bluntly: 'If we do not take steps to maintain the purity of blood, the Jew will destroy civilization by poisoning us all.' The effluent of history. Scarcely human. Grubs.

SAMUELS: *(unfunnily):* He must've met the wife's family.

WATERS: Negroes. Cripples. Defectives. The mad. Women. *(Turning deliberately to* MURRAY's *row.)* Workers. Dirty. Unschooled. Shifty. Grabbing all they can get. Putting coal in the bath. Chips with everything. Chips and beer. Trade Unions dedicated to maximizing wages and minimizing work. Strikes for the idle. Their greed. And their bottomless stupidity. Like children, unfit to look after themselves. Breeding like rabbits, sex-mad. And their mean vicious womenfolk, driving them on. Animals, to be fed slops and fastened up at night. (*Long pause.*) The traitor destroys the truth.

(*Comedians*, act 1)

Shortly after this scene, Samuels, who is Jewish, says "You were having us on. That's a relief. I was beginning to get worried."

The students recognize that Waters was trying to teach them something about humor, and one of the students says "Lesson Three: Stereotypes." And Waters adds, "If I've told you once, I've told you a thousand times. We work *through* laughter, not *for* it." Then Waters points out "It's not the jokes. It's what lies behind 'em. It's the attitude...."

44. *Theme and Variation (logic)*

By theme and variation I refer to the technique comedy writers use to take some matter (a belief, an activity) and show how different nationalities, religions, occupations, members of social classes, etc. vary with regard to this belief or activity. Part of the humor here comes from seeing how the theme is varied by the different groups, and by the way this techniques plays with stereotypes people have of different groups.

In the second act of Trevor Griffiths's *Comedians*, the students are giving a performance of their acts. One of the students, Connor, uses theme and variation in his act. The selection below comes from shortly after the beginning of his act.

CONNOR: ...You know, even the Catholic Church is different here. I went to Mass at the Holy Name, like a bloody opera. Back home in Wexford it's more like a market. The priest charges ten percent commission on all transactions. And confessions...Jesus...here you can hear the candles melt, so you can...your Irish priest is either half-deaf or half-cut, so you've gotta burst your lungs off to get absolution, safact. (*Bellows.*) Bless me, Father, for I have sinned, it is six years since my last confession...(*Own voice.*) *Then* you can hear a pin drop...(*Priest's voice, drunk.*) Speak up, my son, there's nothing to be ashamed of now, the Lord welcomes sinners, big and small...(*Bellows.*) I have missed Mass seven hundred and twenty-three times...I have fornicated.... Yer English priest enjoys it too much...Oh yes. (*English priest's voice, dripping with retracted interest, low and breathy, close to mic.*) Yes, I see, my son, and *you* put your hand where? (*Self, very low, hesitant but intense.*) I put it...down her mouth, father. (*Priest, slight but controlled increase in excitement.*) Did you now? Erm...and why did you do that, my son? (*Self.*) She 'ad dis...bone stuck, father...(*Own voice.*) Or there's the other sort, the feller that's gonna end up Bishop's secretary, he's very bored...(*Bored posh priest, testy*.) All right, so you've been wearing your sister's clothes again, don't you ever do anything else...? Don't you fancy your mother's...? I mean you're in here every week the same story, there's no development, there's no plot, look, it might excite you, there's absolutely nothing in it for me...

(*Comedians*, act 2)

Connor is taking as his theme or subject, the way priests respond to people who are confessing, and offering variations on this theme: the responses of the typical Catholic Priest, English Priest, and bored posh priest. We see other techniques as well, such as insult and revelation.

45. *Unmasking and Pretense (identity)*

In unmasking, we bring to light what someone is trying to conceal (a secret, an identity or whatever). Pretense is the other side of the matter and involves a situation in which a character pretends something (a woman pretends she's a man, or vice versa or a character pretends to be ill) to trick or fool other characters. When there is pretense, a tension is established. Will the pretender be able to fool the other characters or will he or she be unmasked? And if there is an unmasking, how is it accomplished?

Earlier in this discussion of comedic techniques, I dealt with coincidence and used Sheridan's *The School for Scandal* as an example. Joseph Surface is attempting to seduce Lady Teazle when Sir Peter Teazle pays an unexpected visit. Lady Teazle hides behind a screen. While Sir Peter is talking with Joseph, confessing that he fears his wife has formed an attachment to his brother Charles, a servant comes in and announces that Charles has arrived and will be with them shortly. Sir Peter hides in a closet and asks Joseph to quiz his brother about his relationship with Lady Teazle. Joseph tries to suggest that Charles and Lady Teazle are having a relationship and lies about them, but Charles doesn't fall for the bait. Sir Peter comes out and tells him he is relieved. The servant informs Joseph that Lady Sneerwell, who is conspiring with him, is below. Joseph rushes down to speak to her. Sir Peter tells Charles that there's a French milliner behind the screen. Charles pulls down the screen and everyone is startled to find Lady Teazle. Just then, Joseph returns and discovers, to his horror, that they have found Lady Teazle there. He starts making up a story about why she is there—because of his love for Maria—but she refuses to go along with him.

LADY TEAZLE: There is not one syllable of truth in what that gentleman has told you.
SIR PETER: I believe you, upon my soul, ma'am.
JOSEPH: [*Aside to* LADY TEAZLE] 'Sdeath, madam, will you betray me?
LADY TEAZLE: Good Mr. Hypocrite, by your leave, I'll speak for myself.
SIR PETER: Ay, let her alone, sir; you'll find she'll make out a better story than you, without prompting.
LADY TEAZLE: Hear me, Sir Peter!—I came here on no matter relating to your ward, and even ignorant of this gentleman's pretensions to her. But I came, seduced by his insidious arguments, at least to listen to his pretended passion, if not to sacrifice your honour to his baseness.
SIR PETER: Now, I believe, the truth is coming, indeed!

(*The School for Scandal*, act 4, scene 3)

Thus, Joseph Surface is unmasked and revealed to be a hypocrite and villain. The central comedic tension in the story is resolved as Charles triumphs at the end and his brother, Lady Sneerwell and their friends are unmasked and discredited. Unmasking and revelation is a common technique used in comedies and often is the way these works are resolved.

This discussion of unmasking concludes my examination of the forty-five techniques of humor that playwrights use to make people laugh. I will end this theoretical section with discussions of techniques and comedic style, the use of comic techniques in performance and with comic types.

Basic Techniques of Humor Generation and Style

From my perspective, one of the defining aspects of a writer's style is the way he or she uses and combines the various techniques of humor listed above. These techniques, as I have pointed out, are often used in combination. In analyzing a simple text, such as joke, it is quite common to find two or three techniques being used, with one technique dominant and other techniques having secondary status. With this list of techniques, then, it is possible to see how authors generate humor and determine whether an author tends to use certain techniques most of the time and neglect others. This use of particular techniques would give us, then, a more specific understanding of his or her comedic style than was possible before.

If you wish to be mechanistic, you can think of these techniques as "devices" used by authors. I don't believe that authors are generally conscious or fully conscious of the techniques they are using or that they can articulate them with any degree of precision. They create comedy based on a variety of factors, some conscious and others unconscious—what they feel is correct or "works" in a given situation, to generate laughter and do whatever else they wish to do, at the same time. But armed with this catalogue of techniques, we can see what techniques they have favored and unravel, to some degree, the mystery of creating comedy.

On Performance and Theatrical Matters

This book deals with dramatic comedies and thus does not consider the matter of performance, but I would like to say something about it. There is a kind of magic in the way actors and actresses can "become" characters in plays and the way their performances can generate laughter. When we read plays and their stage directions, we can, in our mind's eye, often "see" the performances the authors anticipated. And, in some cases, in which we've seen a play performed, we can remember the way the actors and actresses brought the play to life.

I will list some of the factors involved in performance that can be used to make the lines of a comedy do a better job of generating laughter. Many of these comic ploys involve using various techniques, such as exaggeration and imitation, I might add.

1. *Facial Expression.* Performers can make "funny" faces to create humor, exaggerate their facial responses to lines or actions by other characters and use their faces (eyes, eyebrows, cheeks, lips) to reveal their feelings and attitudes.
2. *Body Language.* Performers can use exaggerated body language to heighten the humor in a given situation. They can jump, they can twist themselves into shapes, they can do "funny walking" and other things as well.
3. *Makeup and Props.* The makeup of performers, their hairstyles and hair color, the clothes they wear and the props they use (their eyeglasses, for instance) all can contribute to the humor by suggesting character and personality. A grotesque character with a white face and a purple nose, like Krapp, has an effect upon people in the audience and colors, literally as well as figuratively, the way they react to the him.
4. *Voice Usage.* The way characters talk—in monotones, in high pitched tones (when men pretend to be women), the accents and dialects they use, and whether they talk very slowly or very quickly, speak correctly or incorrectly, talk gibberish and double-talk—all have comic potentialities.

5. *Noises and Sound Effects.* Here I'm talking about everything from belches and farts by uncouth characters to the use of noises (sirens, buzzers, telephones ringing, etc.) and other sound-effects to heighten dramatic effects.
6. *Scenery.* The scenery can also intensify the comedic possibilities in a script—since it can be used to "reveal" what a character is really like (a slob, a fanatic about cleanliness, an aesthete, a square, a lecher).

A Note on Personality Types in Comedies

Aristotle said that comedy involved "an imitation of men worse than average," of people who are "ridiculous." The humorous characters in comedies often are "types"—monomaniacs, characters with one dominating humor or comic passion. These comic characters often are played off against relatively normal characters—frequently young lovers. They must cope with humorous characters of all sorts and find a way to use and manipulate their ruling passions in order to overcome the various obstacles these monomaniacs create for them.

A list of some of the more common types of humorous stock characters follows below.

1. *Boasters or Alazons.* They appear in everything from Greek comedies to modern day works. One of the most famous is Miles Gloriosus, the boaster (and fool) in Plautus's play *Miles Gloriosus*. He lacks self-understanding and doesn't realize that everyone thinks of him as a fool. He is also a gull—who is naïve and easily persuaded, two common characteristics of fools. I analyze *Miles Gloriosus* in the second chapter of this book.
2. *Pretenders or Eirons.* These characters trick other characters to obtain some goal: money, freedom, a loved one or a lusted-after one, etc. A great deal of comedy involves characters who are dissemblers, pretending something (men pretending they are women, women pretending they are men, kings pretending they are commoners, servants pretending they are helping their masters, and so on). Wily servants are often eirons. Volpone was an eiron figure, and so, it turns out, was his servant Mosca.
3. *Gulls.* They are fooled by the pretenders and are tricked out of something. They are naïve, gullible, easily persuaded to do things, generally because they are both trusting and stupid.
4. *Hicks or Agroikos.* They are country bumpkins who know little of city life, are often gulls, though not always—since there is also the reverse—the convention of the shrewd country type who tricks gullible and naïve city types.
5. *Pedants.* In commedia dell'arte one of the standard characters is the *dottore*, or pedant. These characters always have their nose buried in books and

are unworldly and impractical, full of theoretical knowledge but bumblers who are unable to function in the real world. The stereotype of the absent-minded and unworldly professor comes from the *dottore* figure.
6. *Old Men or Senexes*. Frequently these characters have a beautiful young ward who, often, they wish to marry (or wish to marry off to someone the ward doesn't like) and it is the task of the hero, the male lead, often helped by a shrewd servant or slave (or similar figure) to outwit the *senex* and marry the girl. Sometimes the senex figure is actually married to a young wife and that poses numerous complications: the old husband is jealous, the young wife unsatisfied in various ways and with a different perspective on life.
7. *Fools or Schlemiels*. Fools are people who lack self-knowledge, who are simpletons, who have bad luck, who are misfits, who are gauche, who make stupid bargains (can be gulled), who are born losers and victims. (There are also wise fools in some plays—characters who know and speak the truth and, ironically, aren't listened to, because they are fools.) In Jewish humor there are many schlemiels, who are inept and always spilling soup and when they spill soup, they always do so on characters who are even more gauche, schlamatzls.

There are numerous other comic types such as dandies, fops, misers, misanthropes, sex-starved women and men, gluttons, cynics, and milquetoasts who are found in comedies. The common characteristic of many of these characters is that they are driven by one dominating passion—monomaniacs so to speak—and this ruling passion or monomania can be used to create humorous interactions among the characters.

Comic Techniques and the Study of Comedies

We are now prepared to examine a number of comedies—dramatic works meant to amuse and generate laughter as well as other things, in some cases—in which institutions and social practices are satirized, politically embarrassing events are alluded to, authors are parodied, and famous individuals are ridiculed.

For analysis I have chosen what I consider to be four funny and interesting comedies: Plautus's *Miles Gloriosus* Shakespeare's *Twelfth Night*, Sheridan's *The School for Scandal* and Ionesco's *The Bald Soprano*. I will focus on the comic devices used in the plays, but I will discuss other matters as well—lest I be accused of being a monomaniac with an idée fixe, that techniques are the only thing of importance in comedies. My focus on techniques will give this book a distinctive character and provide those interested in understanding how playwrights create comedy and generate humor an extended analysis of the techniques used to generate humor and an application of those techniques to some of the greatest comedies of world literature.

2

The Braggart Captain: *Miles Gloriosus*

Miles Gloriosus was written by Titus Maccius Plautus, who was born in Sarsina, a town in Umbria, around 254 B.C. and died in 184 B.C. Plautus is said to have written more than 100 plays, but only twenty survive. Twelve "lost comedies" of Plautus were discovered in 1427, which were widely read and studied, frequently performed, and highly influential.

Alazons and *Eirons*

The "hero" of this play, a captain named Pyrgopolinices, is a classic *Alazon* figure—a boaster. Pyrgopolinices is a boaster of awesome proportions, who thinks he is wonderful and worshipped by all, but in reality is looked upon by everyone as a fool and lout. We now use the name of this play generically, and characterize foolish boasters as "Miles Gloriosus types."

Alazons frequently find themselves involved with another classic comic type, *Eirons*—dissemblers, who often pretend to admire and help the *Alazons* but generally devise schemes to discomfort them. In this play that role is played by Palaestrio, a slave of Pyrgopolinices, who thinks up an ingenious way of uniting Philocomasium, a young woman abducted by Pyrgopolineces, with her lover Pleusicles, Palaestrio's former master and preventing them from getting in trouble when they are observed kissing by one of the captain's servants.

The Plot of Miles Gloriosus

Plautus provides us with an excellent summary of the play in his "Argument of the Play" which follows:

> A young Athenian and a free-born courtesan were madly in love with each other. When he left home on an embassy to Naupactus, a soldier falls in with the girl,

and against her will carries her off to Ephesus. The Athenian's servant sets sail to inform his master of this fact; he is captured, however, and as a captive is presented to that self same soldier. He writes to the master to come to Ephesus. The young fellow flies there, and puts up at the house next door with a friend of his father. The servant opens up the wall [secretly] between the two houses so that the lovers may have a private passage way. He pretends that the girl's twin sister has come. Then the master of the house provides Palaestrio with a protégée of his own to cajole the soldier. He is taken in, hopes to marry, dismisses the young woman, and is flogged as an adulterer.

One important thing that Plautus leaves out in his summary is that a servant of the braggart soldier, Sceledrus, supposedly searching for a stray monkey, has seen Philocomasium kissing her lover, Pleusicles, in the neighbor's house. Palaestrio hits upon the idea of creating an imaginary twin sister to convince Sceledrus he has not seen Philocomasium, but instead her twin sister, Glycera. The actress who plays Philocomasium also plays Glycera, and runs back and forth between the two houses, to befuddle Sceledrus. The second part of the play involves convincing Pyrgopolinices to get rid of Philocomasium so he can marry a courtesan. The courtesan, Acroteleutium, has been coached by Palaestrio to pretend to be in love with Pyrgopolinices.

Establishing the Character of Pyrgopolinices

In the first few lines of the play, Plautus establishes Pyrgopolinices' character. He has him say:

> PYRGO: Take ye care that the lustre of my shield is more bright than the rays of the sun are wont to be at the time when the sky is clear; that when occasion comes, the battle being joined, 'mid the fierce ranks right opposite it may dazzle the eyesight of the enemy.

His ego, we see, knows no bounds; he wants his shield brighter than the sun's rays. He is led on by his various servants, such as Artotrogus, a parasite, who, like everyone else, considers him a fool.

Thus, when Pyrgo asks where Artotrogus is, he answers:

> Here he is; he stands close by the hero, valiant and successful, and of princely form. Mars could not dare to style himself a warrior so great, nor compare his prowess with yours.

Artogrogus is suggesting, in a highly exaggerated manner, that Pyrgo is a greater warrior than Mars, the god of war.

Pyrgo responds with some wordplay and more of his pomposity:

> PYRGO: Him *you mean* whom I spared on the Gorgonidonian plains where Battleboomski Mightimercenarimuddlekin, the grandson of Neptune, was the chief commander?

Pyrgo's tying a number of words together is a good example of wordplay and creates a feeling of nonsense. This is followed by a discussion in which Pyrgo's "feats" are continually exaggerated, as Artotrogus leads him on. Artotrogus responds:

> ARTO: I remember him; him, I suppose, you mean with the golden armour, whose legions you puffed away with your breath....

We know how Artotrogus feels because in an aside he says that all the talk is about things that the captain never did and that he is full of vain boasting that is beyond belief.

Let me quote a bit of the dialogue to reveal the way Artotrogus continually exaggerates and inflates things:

> ARTO: Lo! Here am I. I 'troth in what a fashion it was you broke the fore-leg of even an elephant, in India, with your fist.
> PYRGO: How?—the fore-leg?
> ARTO: I meant to say this—the thigh.
> PYRGO: I struck the blow without an effort.

In some dialogue a bit later, Artotrogus discusses the number of men Pyrgo has killed in a battle.

> ARTO: I do remember this. In Cilicia there were a hundred and fifty men, a hundred in Cryphiolathronia, thirty at Sardis, sixty men of Macedon, whom you slaughtered altogether in one day.
> PYRGO: What is the sum total of those men?
> ARTO: Seven thousand.

This kind of dialogue establishes the character of Pyrgopolinices as an incredible boaster, whose grandiosity knows no bounds and who does not recognize when he is being lied to and ridiculed. Thus when Artotrogus tells Pyrgopolinices that all women are in love with him since he is so handsome, Pyrgopolinices responds "'Tis *really* a very great plague to be too handsome a man."

Act I, scene 1, establishes the character of Pyrgopolinices as a boaster, puffed up by his own sense of importance (and aided in that by his servant Artotrogus), and, in addition, a person without any sense of how others see him.

The dialogue about how many men Pyrgopolinices has killed at battle, in which the number keeps getting larger, reminds one of Falstaff's famous "men in buckram" scene in *Henry IV, Part I*, discussed earlier, in which he is telling Hal how he was attacked. Since Hal was one of the attackers, he knows what happened but Falstaff doesn't know this.

PRINCE: What, fought ye with them all?

FALSTAFF: All? I know not what you call all, but if I fought not with fifty of them, I am a bunch of radish! If there were not two or three and fifty upon poor old Jack, then am I no two-legged creature.

PRINCE: Pray God you have not murdered some of them.

FALSTAFF: Nay, that's past praying for. I have peppered two of them. Two am I sure I have paid, two rogues in buckram suits. I tell thee what, Hal, if I tell thee a lie, spit in my face, call me horse. Thou knowest my old ward. Here I lay, and thus I bore my point. Four rogues in buckram let drive at me.

PRINCE: What, four? Thou saidst but two even now.

FALSTAFF: Four, Hall. I told thee four.

POINS: Ay, ay, he said four.

FALSTAFF: These four came all affront and mainly thrust at me. I made me no more ado but took all their seven points in my target, thus.

(Act 2, scene 4)

This technique, of continually adding to the number of attackers killed, is exaggeration with inflation and serves to establish the lack of credibility of the exaggerator or of the gullible believer, which is the case in *Miles Gloriosus*. It is similar to "topping" in tall tale contests except that the topping is done by one person on his or her previous tales.

The Complication

In the prologue to act 2, Palaestrio points out that "Alazon" is the Greek form of "Gloriosus," the Latin term for "braggart" and that Pyrgopolinices is "wherever he goes, the laughing stock of all." Palaestrio then expands on the "argument" and sets everything up for the first part of the play, which involves convincing Pyrgopolinices' servant Sceledrus that the person he saw "toying" with Pleusicles in the adjoining house was not Philocomasium but her twin sister, Glycera. It is a coincidence—by chance, Sceledrus was on the roof and able to see the lovers—that provides the complication in the play.

When Palaestrio learns what has happened he devises this stratagem to trick Sceledrus so that "what was seen may not have been seen." As Palaestrio puts it, "I shall say that her own twin-sister has come here from Athens, with a certain person, her lover, to Philocomasium, as like to *her* as milk is to milk."

He then meets Sceledrus, who tells him what he has seen. Palaestrio warns Sceledrus that he is in trouble, for if he falsely accuses Philocomasium he will be undone, and if he is correct, since he was supposed to be guarding her, he will also be undone. What follows are a number of scenes in which Palaestrio and Philocomasium dupe Sceledrus. He does not know that there is a secret passageway between the two houses (the technique used here is "ignorance") and thus when Philocomasium is shown to be at home, and another woman looking like Philocomasium is shown to be in the neighbor's house, Sceledrus assumes that there are, indeed, twin sisters, and he has not seen Philocomasium toying with her lover but her twin sister Glycera.

After Palaestrio has met Sceledrus, and learned what Sceledrus has seen, Palaestrio starts the plot in motion. Sceledrus is told to stand watch on the neighbor's house while Palaestrio goes into Pyrgopolinices' house to fetch Philocomasium. While in the house he coaches her on what she is to do, so they can fool Sceledrus. Palaestrio emerges from Pyrgopolinices' house with Philocomasium. Let me quote some lines here to give the flavor of the scene:

SCEL: [*Looking*] O ye immortal Gods, it really is the lady of my master!
PAL: I' faith, so she seems to me as well. Do then, now, since you would have it—
SCEL: Do what?
PAL: Die this very instant.
PHIL: [*Advancing*] Where is this faithful servant, who has falsely accused me in my innocence of this most heinous crime?
PAL: See, here he is; 'tis he that told me,—assuredly 'twas he.
PHIL: Villain, did you say that you had seen me next door kissing?

But Sceledrus holds fast and says, a few lines later, "I shall never be intimidated from having seen what I *really* did see."

Then Philocomasium, having been coached by Palaestrio, tells the dream she had that night.

> PHIL: Last night, in my sleep, my twin sister seemed to have come from Athens to Ephesus with a certain person, her lover. Both of them seemed to me to be having their lodgings here next door.
>
> PAL: [*To the Audience*] The dream that's being related is Palaestrio's—*pray,* go on.
>
> PHIL: I seemed to be delighted because my sister had come, *and*, on her account I seemed to be incurring a most grievous suspicion. For, in my sleep, my own servant seemed to accuse me, as you *are* now *doing*, of being caressed by a strange young man, whereas it was that own twin-sister of mine, who had been toying with her own friend. Thus did I dream that I was wrongfully accused of a crime.

She then goes into Pyrgopolinices' house. Sceledrus starts having doubts about what he has seen. He knows she is in his master's house and stands guard. Palaestrio plays the role of the friend and counselor to Sceledrus. If the captain finds out about what has happened, Palaestrio says, "you certainly are undone." Sceledrum is beginning to crack.

> SCEL: Not a word of certainty have I to utter; I did not see her, although I did see her.

Philocomasium then changes her clothes, goes to the neighbor's house, and comes out of it. Sceledrus sees her and is astonished. They approach her and Sceledrus asks her what she was doing in the neighbor's house. Philocomasium doesn't answer (since she is pretending she doesn't know either of them, because she is Glycera, Philcomasium's twin sister.)

> SCEL: I am addressing you, *woman*, brimful of viciousness and disgrace, who are roaming about among your neighbors.
> PHIL: To whom are you talking?
> SCEL: To whom but to yourself?
> PHIL: What person are you? Or what business have you with me?
> SCEL: O, you ask me who I am, do you?
> PHIL: Why shouldn't I ask that which I don't know.

This leads to an amusing bit of dialogue between Palaestrio and Sceledrus about whether they are themselves or have been transformed into someone else without knowing it. They decide they are still themselves and then continue their discussion with Philcomasium.

She then tells them her name is Glycera and that she just arrived the evening before from Athens with her lover. Sceledrus grabs her and tells her to go into Pyrgo's house, and she says she's going to the house where she belongs. When Sceledrus lets go of her she runs into the house of Periplectomenus, the neighbor of Pyrgopolinices. Palaestrio convinces Sceledrus to get him a sword, from Pyrgopolinices' house, knowing that Sceledrus will find Philocomasium there, lying on a sofa. He returns saying he has seen his mistress and that, indeed, he would have been undone if he had told Pyrgo about the matter.

Palaestrio warns Sceledrus that he still is in considerable trouble, since he has annoyed Glycera. "If you're wise, you'll hold your tongue. It befits a servant to know of more than he speaks." To make certain that Sceledrus is duped, Periplectomenus comes out of his house and chats with Sceledrus, telling him that he will probably be severely beaten for having broken his tiles and having accused his guest, Glycera, of criminality. Periplectomenus then commands Sceledrus to go into his house and see Glycera. Periplectomenus then tells Philocomasium to go into his house, and after Sceledrus has seen her there, to return to the Pyrgopolinices' house.

Sceledrum goes into Periplectomenus' house, where he sees Philocomasium. He returns and we find the following dialogue:

SCEL: I *certainly* merit chastisement.
PERIP: What then? Is it she?
SCEL: Although 'tis she, 'tis not she.
PERIP: Have you seen this Lady?
SCEL: I have seen both her and *the gentleman*, your guest, caressing and kissing.
PERIP: Is it she?
SCEL: I know not.
PERIP: Would you know for certain?
SCEL: I *should* like to.
PERIP: Go you this instant into your house: see whether your lady is within.
SCEL: Very well: you've advised me rightly. I'll be out again to you this instant. [*Goes into the* CAPTAIN's *house.*]
PERIP: I' faith, I never saw any man more cleverly fooled, and by singular devices. But here he is coming.

Sceledrus is now convinced that he had made a mistake and, being scared of what might happen when his master returns, decides to hide.

On the Singular Devices of Comedy

I would like to discuss, in some detail, the comic devices that Plautus has used in this play—up to this point.

1. *Eccentricity.* I use the term broadly to deal with characters who are ridiculous (as Aristotle would put it) "types," who are one-dimensional and, in a humorous sense, monomaniacs. Thus, the captain, is a braggart (or *Alazon*) who is also a fool. Eccentric characters can be ridiculed with ease and made to be foolish and objects of laughter.
2. *Revelation of Ignorance.* Here I refer to Pyrgopolinices' lack of knowledge about what he really is like and how people feel about him; he thinks he is loved by all whereas they consider him a fool. The fact that Sceledrus did not know of the tunnel connecting the two houses makes it possible for him to be duped. A great deal of comedy involves characters who are unaware of something and can be misled.
3. *Coincidences.* It was a coincidence that Philocomasium and Palaestrio ended up at the household of Pyrgopolinices. It was also a coincidence that Sceledrus saw Philocomasium and Pleusicles kissing and "toying" with one another. These coincidences make it possible for the plot to work out the way it does.
4. *Impersonation.* The first part of the play involves everyone duping Sceledrus. This is done by having Philocomasium play two roles: herself and her make-believe twin sister, Glycera. It was possible for her to do this because there was a secret passageway between the captain's house and his neighbor's house, but she also had to pretend to be two different persons.
5. *Mistakes.* Palaestrio has to convince Sceledrus that he had made a mistake, and used the device of impersonation to do so. Sceledrus was able to be convinced because he was ignorant (and didn't know about the secret passage) and because logic tells us that one person cannot be in two separate places at the same time. He is ultimately persuaded, then, that his eyes did deceive him and that he saw Glycera and not Philocomasium.
6. *Analogy.* The dream that Philocomasium told Sceledrus was devised to present what could possibly have happened, and thus helped him come to the conclusion that he had made a mistake and didn't see what he actually saw. It planted an idea in his head that led him to believe that he had been mistaken.
7. *Wordplay.* The zany and ridiculous line about "Battleboomski Mightimercenarimuddlekin, the grandson of Neptune," involves wordplay, as Plautus ties together mighty and mercenary and muddle into one long word.

8. *Absurdity*. There are a number of lines in which Sceledrus speaks in a paradoxical and self-contradictory way. Some examples would be "I did not see her, although I did see her" and "although 'tis she, 'tis not she." This technique, of uttering contradictions, is humor of the absurd in my typology.
9. *Insult*. In a number of the asides, characters tell what they really think of Pyrgopolinices. These are indirect insults but insults nonetheless.
10. *Comparison*. In one scene Pyrgopolinices compares himself to Achilles, showing his boundless ego. It is the extreme exaggeration of the comparison here that generates the humor.
11. *Irony*. Palaestrio is an *eiron*, a dissembler, who uses his intelligence to free Philocomasium. The play is driven by dramatic comedic irony, since Palaestrio seems to be helping Sceledrus and Pyrgopolinices whereas, in reality, he is duping them.
12. *Embarrassment*. Escape from embarrassment is a common theme in comedy. In *Miles Gloriosus* Sceledrus is in a position to embarrass Philocomasium, unless he can be convinced that he made a mistake. The first part of the play deals with this matter and the second part deals with springing Philocomasium free.

The humor in this play is accessible to modern audiences, since Plautus does not do much in the way of wordplay, doesn't parody authors we are not familiar with and doesn't make allusions to events that modern audiences don't know about.

A Philosophical Digression on Love, Marriage, and Family Relationships

The last three acts of the play (acts 3, 4, and 5) involve convincing Pyropolinices that a beautiful courtesan is in love with him, so he should send Philocomasium away. There is a wonderful scene in which Pleusicles, Palaestrio, and Periplectomenus have a philosophical discourse on the nature of love and marriage. Periplectomenus says he devotes himself to "pleasure, love, and mirth," and that he prefers to remain single.

PERIP: I could have married a dowered wife of the best family; but I don't choose to introduce an *everlasting* female barker at me into my house.

PLEUS: Why don't you choose? For 'tis a delightful thing to be the father of children.

PERIP: Troth, 'tis very much sweeter by far to be free yourself. For a good wife, if it is possible for her to be married anywhere on earth, where can I find her? But am I to take one home who is never to say this to me, "Buy me some wool, my dear, with which a soft and warm cloak can be made, and good winter under-clothes, that you mayn't catch cold from this winter-weather"; such as this you can never hear from a wife, but, before the cock's crow, she awakes me from my sleep, *and* says, "Give me *some money*, my dear, with which to make my mother a present on the Calends, give me *some money* to make preserves, give me something to give on the Quinquatrus to the sorceress....

Pleusicles replies that a person of wealth and stature such as Periplectomenus should have children as "a memorial of his race and of himself."

Periplectomenus counters that he has many relatives and has no need of children. He then offers a short disquisition on families, human nature and greed.

PERIP: For I shall bequeath my property to my relations, *and* divide it among them. These, like children, pay attentions to me; they come to see how I do, or what I want; before it is daybreak they are with me; they make inquiry how I have enjoyed my sleep in the night. Them will I have for children who are *ever* sending presents to me...They vie with one another with their presents; I say in a low voice to myself: "They are gaping after my property; while, in their emulations, they are nourishing me and loading me with presents."

PAL: Upon right good grounds and right well do you fully understand yourself and your own interests, and if you are happy, sons twofold and threefold have you.

(Act 3, scene 2)

This bit of dialogue is a somewhat cynical view of human relationships (though there's an element of truth to it) and is, as it turns out, the basis of *Volpone*, Jonson's brilliant comedy that was written some 1800 years later.

The talk then turns to how Philocomasium might be rescued and Palaestrio has a scheme. It involves Periplectomenus finding a courtesan, a woman "whose mind and body are full of merriment and subtlety" to pretend she is his wife. She will pretend to fall in love with Pyrgopolinices, who will then send Philocomasium away, since she complicates matters. The courtesan is named Acroteleutium and her maid, who participates in the ruse, is Milphidippa. Palaestrio serves as the go-between and advisor to Pyrgopolinices.

We find Palaestrio laying the groundwork for the scheme in act 4, scene 1. He tells the captain about a handsome woman who loves him, and gives him a ring that Periplectomenus lent him.

The Braggart Captain: *Miles Gloriosus*   61

PYRGO: What's this? Whence comes it?

PAL: From a charming and a handsome lady, one who loves you and dotes upon your extreme beauty. Her maid just now gave me the ring that I might then give it to you.

He explains that it comes from the wife of Periplectomenus, who hates him and is dying for Pyrgopolinices.

PYRGO: What shall we do with that mistress *of mine*, who is at my house?

PAL: Why, do you bid her to be gone about her business, wherever she chooses; as her twin-sister has come to Ephesus, and her mother, and they are come to fetch her.

(Act 4, scene 1)

Pyrgopolinices sees this as a "charming opportunity to turn the wench out of doors," and falls for the trick. Palaestrio suggests she be turned out very handsomely and allowed to keep the gold and trinkets Pyrgopolinices had given her and he agrees.

The remainder of the play involves having the courtesan and her maid actually gull the captain, Pyrgopolinices. He has a talk with Philocomasium and "convinces" her to leave him. She asks to be given Palaestrio, along with her jewelry and gold and the captain agrees. In the scene that follows, the courtesan and her maid carry on a conversation in a very loud voice about how wonderful Pyrgopolinices is, so he can overhear them. The following conversation then takes place:

PYRGO: How I do seem to be loved.

PAL: You are deserving of it....

ACROT: [*Aloud*] Troth, if he shall refuse to take me as his wife, by heavens I'll embrace his knees and entreat him! If I shall be unable to prevail on him, in some way or other, I'll put myself to death. I'm quite sure that without him I cannot live.

(Act 4, scene 6)

The captain wants to go to Acroteleutium immediately, but Palaestrio advises him to hold back and let her come to him and try to win him. The courtesan and her maid continue their conversation, making sure they are overheard by the captain, talking about how wonderful he is.

PAL: [*To* PYRGOPOLINICES] No doubt all of the women, as soon as each has seen you, are in love with you.

> PYRGO: [*To* PALAESTRIO] I don't know whether you have heard it or not; I'm the grandson of Venus.
>
> (Act 4, scene 6)

His inability to see that he is being put on and his incredible vanity are the source of the humor here.

The courtesan's maid comes and invites her to join the courtesan in Periplectomenus's house. The maid says that the courtesan has turned her husband out of the house and that he gave her the house as her marriage-portion. This scene is followed by one in which Pleusicles, disguised as a seaman, comes to fetch Philocomasium, to take her, her twin sister and her mother back to Athens. She pretends to be devastated about having to leave the captain, but leaves. Palaestrio says good-bye to the captain.

> PAL: Consider every now and then how faithful I have been to you. If you do that, then at last you'll know who is honest towards you and who dishonest.
>
> (Act 5, scene 1)

He then leaves.

Pyrgopolinices enters the house of his neighbor and falls into the trap that was set for him. Periplectomenus has his servants beat the captain and pretends to be angry.

> PERIP: Why have you dared, disgraceful fellow, to seduce another man's wife?
> PYRGO: So may the Gods bless me, she came to me of her own accord.
>
> (Act 5, scene 1)

Periplectomenus then tells his servants to castrate Pyrgopolinices, who pleads that he was told by Acroteleuteum's maid that she was a widow. Periplectomenus makes the captain take an oath that he won't injure anyone because of the affair, which he does.

In the last scene, Pyrgopolinices asks Sceledrus whether Philocomasium has sailed away yet. Sceledrus then says that he saw the sailor kissing Philocomasium once they got outside the city gates. The captain recognizes, then, that he'd been duped.

> PYRGO: O wretched *fool* that I am! I see that I have been gulled. That scoundrel of a fellow, Palaestrio, it was he that contrived this plot against me.
>
> (Act 5, scene 2)

Sceledrus comments on how well the plot was handled and he and his master go into the captain's house. An actor asks the audience for applause and with that the play ends.

The play has a set of polar oppositions that give it meaning. These oppositions revolve around illusion and reality and are sketched out below:

ILLUSION	REALITY
Pyrgopolinices	**Palaestrio**
Fool and Braggart	Schemer and Pretender
Gullibility	Manipulation
Pomposity	Deflation
Alazon figure	*Eiron* figure
Literalness	Irony
False lover	True lover
Acroteleteum	**Philocomasium**

By the time the captain recognizes that he has been duped, it is too late—the lovers have been united and set sail for home.

A Final Note on the Techniques of Humor

The second half of the play involves duping the captain and convincing him that he should cast off Philocomasium and take on a new lover. He is a bit hesitant about this, and about getting involved with a formerly married woman, but his gullibility and his ego convince him to do so. Thus, we have a repeat of some of the techniques used in the first part of the play: gullibility and the revelation of ignorance. There are several other techniques I would like to discuss here.

1. *Flattery (Reversal of Insult).* The characters continually flatter the captain, and he accepts this flattery because of his egotism and because he is a fool. He doesn't recognize he is being flattered and responds, after being told that all women who see him love him, by saying that he is a grandson of Venus, the goddess of beauty.
2. *Slapstick.* The captain is beaten and threatened with castration—matters that involve a considerable amount of physical action. There is also a scene in which he struts about, seemingly full of "disdain," after hearing about how much he is loved.

3. *Misunderstanding.* In several bits of dialogue, Palaestrio uses words ambiguously. He says things that are understood by the captain one way, but if we look closely at his words, can be taken a different way.

Conclusions

Miles Gloriosus, though written more than two thousand years ago, still "works" as a comedy and is extremely funny. The plot, like many comedies, is based on intrigue and trickery, and is rather complex. In essence, some characters find themselves in a "mess" and have to figure a way to get out of it. Having a fool to contend with and a clever servant who is a "master-plotter" makes things easier. The play, like many comedies, revolves around the polarities of illusion and reality or trust and deception, and, as is often the case in comedies, deals with the ways in which lovers who are separated and have obstacles to overcome do so and find a way to get together.

3

Make What You Will of Comedy: *Twelfth Night*

Twelfth Night is generally considered one of Shakespeare's greatest romantic comedies, if not his greatest one. Even though it was written in (or about) 1600, almost four hundred years ago, it still has the power to generate enormous laughter in audiences. One of the possible sources for the plot of *Twelfth Night* is Plautus, who used the device of a woman pretending to be her twin sister to great effect in *Miles Gloriosus*. In *Twelfth Night*, as in *Miles Gloriosus*, identity is a major consideration and identity confusion, along with gender confusion, is an important comic element. One of the female leads is Viola, a woman (who has an identical twin brother, Sebastian) who pretends to be a young man, Cesario.

It is the ninth of his comedies and his twentieth play. The title, *Twelfth Night*, refers to the twelve days of festivity and revelry celebrating Christmas and functioning as a prologue to Epiphany. The subtitle, *or, What You Will*, suggests license and freedom, and perhaps (to give a more contemporary interpretation to matters) the power of the readers and viewers of the play to invent their *own* title and, as reader-response critics would argue, make of it what they can and participate in the "creation" of the text.

Introducing the Characters

The first scenes introduce us to the main characters. In act 1, scene 1, Orsino (in Italian, Little Bear) is shown to be a lovesick suitor, smitten with Olivia, who spurns his love and says she will spurn the company and sight of men, in memory of her recently deceased brother. It is a matter of love at first sight on the part of the Duke:

DUKE: Oh, when mine eyes did see Olivia first,
Methought she purged the air of pestilence!
That instant was I turned into a hart.

(Act 1, scene 1)

Olivia, unfortunately for the Duke, is not only mourning her dead brother, but also does not like Orsino and wants nothing to do with him.

In scene 2, we meet Viola and a captain. She has been in a shipwreck and believes, mistakenly it turns out, that her twin brother Sebastian has been drowned. There is an interesting parallel here: one of the female leads has a dead brother and the other female lead thinks she has a dead brother. The captain tells her they are in Illyria and recounts the story of Orsino's love for Olivia and the way she spurns him. Viola decides to disguise herself as a young boy, Cesario, and enter the service of Orsino.

VIOLA: Conceal me what I am, and be my aid
For such disguise as haply shall become
The form of my intent. I'll serve this Duke.
Thou shall present me as eunuch to him.

(Act 1, scene 2)

We move in the next scene, scene 3, to Olivia's house, where we encounter Maria, Olivia's chambermaid; Sir Toby Belch, Olivia's dissolute uncle; and Sir Andrew Aguecheek, a gullish fool who is led on by Sir Toby and thinks himself a creditable suitor to Olivia. His character is described for us by Maria, who in conversation with Sir Toby says that Sir Andrew's a fool and a spendthrift. Sir Toby counters that Sir Andrew speaks three or four languages and "hath all the good gifts of nature."

MARIA: He hath indeed, almost natural, for besides that he's a fool, he's a great quarreler. And but that he hath the gift of a coward to allay the gust he hath in quarreling, 'tis thought among the prudent he would quickly have the gift of a grave.

(Act 1, scene 3)

In the next few scenes we meet the rest of the main characters: Feste, the clown (a professional fool—that is, one who plays the role of a fool—unlike Sir Andrew, who is a natural or "real" fool); Malvolio, Olivia's steward, who is full of self-love and absurd ambitions (to marry Olivia); and assorted servants of Olivia and attendants of the Duke. These first scenes are full of wordplay and other comic devices.

Names of the Characters

The names of a number of the characters in the play are suggestive. In literary works, the names of characters often have a symbolic significance and meaning, and this holds true in *Twelfth Night*, as many of the characters have names that mean something. Let me list the names and say something about the possible or probable meanings:

Orsino means little bear. *Orso* means bear and "ino" is a diminutive in Italian;

Malvolio is close to the Italian *mal voglio* or, loosely, bad wishes or bad will;

Aguecheek has the word *ague*, or fever, in it so an Aguecheek would have red (as in one with a fever) cheeks.

Belch is a gross sound caused by the digestive system.

Feste is close to *festival* or *festivity* and can be connected with the notions of happiness, gaiety, etc.

Fabian comes from a Roman general who obtained victory by delaying battle and harassing his enemies.

It doesn't make sense to push the meanings of these names too far, but it is interesting to note that many of the characters in the play do have names that mean something or have interesting connotations.

Wordplay and the Uses of Language

When Curio, one of the Duke's attendants, asks him whether he wants to go hunting, Orsino doesn't quite hear him, and asks him what he said.

DUKE: What, Curio?
CURIO: The hart.
DUKE: Why, so I do, the noblest that I have.
Oh, when mine eyes did see Olivia first.

Later on, he uses the term "flock" (as in flock of harts) which is a play by Shakespeare upon the hart/heart sound similarity. We also find soundplay in Viola's comment, when she finds she is in Illyria.

VIOLA: What country, friends, is this?
CAPTAIN: This is Illyria, lady.
VIOLA: My brother he is in Elysium.

In act 1, scene 3, Sir Toby introduces Sir Andrew to Maria, Olivia's chambermaid, and says "Accost, Sir Andrew, accost."

SIR ANDREW: What's that?
SIR TOBY: My niece's chambermaid.
SIR ANDREW: Good Mistress Accost, I desire better acquaintance.
MARY: My name is Mary, sir.
SIR ANDREW: Good Mistress Mary Accost—
SIR TOBY: You mistake, knight. "Accost" is front her, board her, woo her, assail her.

This is an example, technically speaking, of misunderstanding rather than mistake, since we are dealing with a confusion about words. Sir Toby is telling Sir Andrew to introduce himself and make a play for her, but he thinks Maria's name is Accost.

When she begins to leave, Sir Andrew says "...Fair lady, do you think you have fools in hand?" To which Mary replies, "Sir, I have not you by the hand," suggesting, in effect, that Sir Andrew is a fool. This is an insult, but Sir Andrew is too stupid to realize it.

SIR ANDREW: Marry, but you shall have, and here's my hand.
MARIA: Now, sir, "thought is free." I pray you, bring your hand to the buttery bar and let it drink.
SIR ANDREW: Wherefore, sweetheart? What's your metaphor?

(Act 1, scene 3)

Her suggestion that he bring his hand to "the buttery bar and let it drink" is an invitation to flirt with her, but he is too stupid to recognize the implication.

Feste and the Abuses of Logic

Shortly after this, we find a scene in which the clown, Feste, and Maria are chatting. She chastises him for being away for a long time and says he may be hanged or sent away. She leaves after telling him to "Make your excuse wisely...."

CLOWN: Wit, an't by thy will, put me into good fooling! Those wits that think they have thee do very oft prove fools, and I that am sure I lack thee may pass for a wise man. For what says Quinapalus? "Better a witty fool than a foolish wit."

(Act 1, scene 5)

He makes an allusion, here, to Quinapalus, Rabelais' clown who was famous for his mock learning. And Feste plays with words, using reversal, and more technically speaking chiasmus, to switch "witty fool" to "foolish wit."

Then he encounters Olivia, who doesn't want to bother with him.

OLIVIA: Go to, you're a dry fool, I'll no more of you. Besides, you grow dishonest.

CLOWN: Two faults, madonna, that drink and good counsel will amend. For give the dry fool drink, then is the fool not dry. Bid the dishonest man mend himself; if he mend, he is no longer dishonest....

(Act 1, scene 5)

Feste is, however, able to avoid being sent away and draws Olivia into a conversation.

CLOWN: Good madonna, why mournest thou?
OLIVIA: Good fool, for my brother's death.
CLOWN: I think his soul is in Hell, madonna.
OLIVIA: I know his soul is in Heaven, fool.
CLOWN: The more fool, madonna, to mourn for your brother's soul being in Heaven. Take away the fool, gentlemen.

(Act 1, scene 5)

In a later scene, act 3, scene 1, Cesario encounters Feste with a tabor or small drum in Olivia's garden and we find some excellent wordplay.

VIOLA: Save thee, friend, and thy music. Doest thou live by thy tabor.
FESTE: No, sir, I live by the church.
VIOLA: Art thou a churchman?
FESTE: No such matter, sir. I do live by the church, for I do live at my house, and my house doth stand by the church....
VILLA: They that dally nicely with words may quickly make them wanton.
FESTE: I would, therefore, my sister had no name, sir.
VIOLA: Why, man?
FESTE: Why, sir, her name's a word, and to dally with that word might make my sister wanton...

Feste jousts with Viola a bit more and then explains that he is not Olivia's fool but something else.

FESTE: I am indeed not her fool, but her corrupter of words.

And that is, to a great measure, what Feste does best—play with words, manipulate them, use them for his purposes, and, in so doing, make sport with logic. "Words," he says, "are grown so false I am loathe to prove reason with them."

Shakespeare offers a disquisition on jesting as, after Feste leaves, Viola speculates on all the things that must be done by a person who plays the fool. The fool or professional wit has to observe, with great care, the mood of his audience. Being a fool or comedian is, she concludes, "As full of labor as a wise man's art."

Feste's creates humor by using or perhaps manipulating logic, and suggesting that since Olivia's brother's soul is in heaven, she has no reason to mourn his death. A set of oppositions is created:

Life	Death
Think	Know
Hell	Heaven
Mourning	Peacefulness

Feste, a professional fool, plays with logic and language throughout *Twelfth Night*. He uses puns and wordplay, overliteralness, facetiousness, ridicule, and various other techniques. In a scene at the end of the play, he impersonates a clergyman, Sir Topas, and tries to convince Malvolio that darkness is light—but impersonation is a deviation from his basic methods, unless you want to argue that playing Feste is, itself, an impersonation.

CLOWN: Sayest thou that house is dark?
MALVOLIO: As Hell, Sir Topas.
CLOWN: Why, it hath bay windows transparent as barricadoes, and the clerestories toward the south-north as lustrous as ebony—and yet complainest thou of obstruction.
MALVOLIO: I am not mad, Sir Topas. I say to you this house is dark.
CLOWN: Madman, thou errest. I say, there is no darkness but ignorance, in which thou art more puzzled than the Egyptians in their fog.

(Act 4, scene 2)

Actually, Malvolio really is in a "fog" for he doesn't know that the letter he found was written by Maria and not Olivia; Feste is therefore speaking the truth, even though he seems to be dissembling.

The Problem of Identity

The central comedic "problem" in the play involves identity. Viola cross-dresses and pretends to be a young male, who becomes a member of Orsino's household; in this "transvestite" role, she fools Orsino, who comments on how "feminine" she is and she fools Olivia, who falls in love with her. She, in turn, has fallen in love with Orsino. We thus have a triangle of lovers with "impossible" loves:

1. Orsino loves Olivia, who spurns him.
2. Olivia falls in love with Cesario, who is really a woman, Viola.
3. Viola falls in love with Orsino, who loves Olivia and who thinks, also, that Viola is a young boy.

Readers of the play or members of the audience know what is going on, but the characters don't.

The first part of the triangle is not connected with identity but with disappointment: a hopeless love. But the second and third parts of the triangle involve the humor of identity, and, in particular, impersonation—a commonly used technique. Two of the characters in this triangle are ignorant of what is going on. Orsino, lovesick over Olivia, imagines that eventually she will respond to his overtures, or those of his messengers. He also believes Viola to be a youth, Cesario. Olivia does not realize that Cesario is really a woman, pretending to be a man.

Viola describes the situation in a celebrated speech:

> VIOLA: Disguise, I see thou art a wickedness,
> Wherein the pregnant enemy does much.
> How easy is it for the proper-false
> In women's waxen hearts to set their forms!
> Alas, our frailty is the cause, not we!
> For such as we are made of, such we be.
> How will this fadge? My master loves her dearly;
> And I, poor monster, fond as much on him,
> As she, mistaken, seems to dote on me.
> What will become of this? As I am man,
> My state is desperate for my master's love;
> As I am woman—now alas the day!—
> What thriftless sighs shall poor Olivia breathe!
> O Time, though must untangle this, not I!
> It is too hard a knot for me to untie! [Exit]
>
> (Act 2, scene 2)

This is the central complication of the play, a "knot" that Viola is not able to untie. It will be untied or, perhaps, cut, in time, when Sebastian arrives on the scene and "ties the knot," so to speak, with Olivia, who thinks she is marrying Cesario. Viola can then reveal that she impersonated a male and can marry Orsino. Everything is resolved at the end of the play when Orsino discovers that Cesario is not a boy, but a woman impersonating a boy. He decides to marry her.

> DUKE: Cesario, come—
> For so you shall be, while you are a man.
> But when in other habits you are seen,
> Orsino's mistress and his fancy's Queen.
> (Act 5, scene 1)

In my glossary I have described this matter of characters not knowing what is going on as ignorance. Some use the term *discrepant awareness* to suggest that certain characters are unaware of what other characters are doing or who they really are, or what is going on in the play. We find that this kind of ignorance, or discrepant awareness, plays a major role in comedies with characters who impersonate other characters or members of a different sex, but discrepant awareness is also found in many other types of comedies. The gap between what the audience knows and what the characters know, provides us with a sense of superiority, among other things. I will have more to say about discrepant awareness shortly.

Technically speaking, the humor of identity (and, more specifically, the technique of impersonation) is always connected with the humor of logic—Orsino and Olivia make mistakes about the gender of Cesario, and, later, Sir Andrew Aguecheek, Sir Toby, and Olivia mistake Sebastian for Cesario.

The Importance of Appearances

Appearances and mistakes are crucial in the play. Orsino has fallen in love with Olivia at first sight. Olivia falls in love with Cesario the same way.

> OLIVIA: Even so quickly may one catch the plague?
> Methinks I feel this youth's perfections
> With an invisible and subtle stealth
> To creep in at mine eyes. Well, let it be.
> (Act 1, scene 4)

And at the end of the play when Olivia encounters Sebastian, who she thinks is Cesario, she asks him whether he will marry her and he, without a moment's pause, agrees to the marriage. This can only be due to love at first sight. In the same light, Orsino says to Cesario, "But when in other habits you are seen," when she puts on her "woman's weeds" and he sees her as a woman, then he will marry her.

There is reason to suggest that Orsino, subconsciously, recognized that Cesario might have been a woman. When we are introduced to Viola in a man's attire, the Duke comments on how feminine Cesario is.

> DUKE: They say thou art a man. Diana's lip
> Is not more smooth and rubious; thy small pipe
> Is as the maiden's organ, shrill and sound,
> And all is semblative a woman's part.
>
> (Act 1, scene 4)

And Malvolio, when asked by Olivia to describe Cesario gives a similar description.

> MALVIOLO: Not yet old enough for a man, nor young enough for a boy, as a squash is before 'tis a peascod, or a codling when 'tis almost an apple. 'Tis with him in standing water, between boy and man. He is very well-favored and he speaks very shrewishly. One would think his mother's milk were scarce out of him.
>
> (Act 1, scene 4)

Shakespeare is playing with the characters, who sense there is something very feminine about the youth, but are deceived by Viola's disguise.

When Olivia asks Cesario whether he is a "comedian" or actor, Viola's reply is misleading:

> VIOLA: No, my profound heart. And yet, by the very fangs of malice I swear, I am not that I play.
>
> (Act 1, scene 5)

In a different scene, Viola tells Orsino the same thing.

> VIOLA: I am all the daughters of my father's house...
>
> (Act 1, scene 4)

But this line is misinterpreted since Cesario is seen by all as a youthful male. This is another example of discrepant awareness or ignorance, which leads characters to interpret truthful statements incorrectly.

There is another aspect of identity to be considered, which doesn't involve impersonation but imitation—namely the matter of a letter that Maria writes, imitating (that is, forging) Olivia's handwriting, that leads to several brilliantly comic scenes and Malvolio's eventual incarceration as a madman. It is to this great comic encounter, one of the greatest in dramatic comedy, that we now turn.

Malvolio's Fantasy

Malvolio is presented as an unsympathetic figure—an unpleasant, puritanical, self-absorbed fool, with delusions of grandeur. Although he has appeared earlier in the play, it is in act 1, scene 5 that we really get to know him. He is to be victimized by a practical joke concocted by Maria. She has imitated Olivia's handwriting and forged a letter to Malvolio, which she leaves in a place that she knows he will find it. The letter could not succeed, of course, unless Malvolio were so foolish and self-deluded as to believe that Olivia would have actually written it to him.

The scene (discussed earlier in this book) starts with Malvolio strutting about, speculating on fortune. He is being observed by Sir Toby, Sir Andrew, Fabian and Maria, who are all hidden.

> MALVIOLIO: 'Tis but fortune, all is fortune. Maria once told me she did affect me. And I have heard herself come this near, that, should she fancy, it should be one of my complexion.

Malvolio is fantasizing about Olivia being in love with him. As he speculates, the various characters who are hiding make comments to one another.

> MALVOLIO: To be Count Malvolio.
> SIR TOBY: Ah, rogue.
> SIR ANDREW: Pistol him, pistol him.
> SIR TOBY: Peace, peace!
> MALVIOLIO: There is example for 't. The lady of Strachy married the yeoman of the wardrobe.

Malvolio then fantasizes on what it would be like married to Olivia. I will tie together the rest of his lines—which are intertwined in the play with comments by Sir Toby, Sir Andrew, and Maria—to give the full flavor of his fantasy:

MALVOLIO: Having been three months married to her, sitting in my state—Calling my officers about me, in my branched velvet gown, having come from a daybed, where I have left Olivia sleeping. And then to have the humor of state. And after a demure travel of regard, telling them I know my place as I would they should do theirs, to ask for my kinsman Toby—Seven of my people, with an obedient start, make out for him. I frown the while, and perchance wind up my watch, or play with my—some rich jewel. Toby approaches, curtsies there to me. I extend my hand to him thus, quenching my familiar smile with an austere regard of control—Saying, "Cousin Toby, my fortunes having cast me on your niece, give me this prerogative of speech— You must amend your drunkenness. Besides, you waste the treasure of your time with a foolish knight—One Sir Andrew.

Shakespeare uses a considerable number of comic devices here in a brilliant manner.

For one thing, Malvolio's secret and erotic fantasies are being revealed to us and to his enemies, and we can laugh at the ridiculous nature of these fantasies—as Malvolio, a steward, dreams of marrying his mistress and becoming a count. This is the technique of *revelation*.

His description of himself in an embroidered velvet gown, a costume much above his station, is both fantastic and a breach of decorum, for commoners were not allowed to be dressed in this manner. Marjorie Garber has suggested in *Vested Interests: Cross-Dressing and Cultural Anxiety* that:

> *Twelfth Night* is a play as much concerned with status as with gender, and its masquerade centers on not one but two cross-dressers: Viola in her male attire, and Malvolio, imagining himself in his "branch'd velvet gown"—ornamented with an embroidered pattern of leafy branches, an elaborate fashion explicitly forbidden to all persons below the rank of knight in sumptuary statutes from the Yorkist period through the time of Elizabeth—before his final, humiliating appearance in cross-gartered yellow stockings. Malvolio, in other words, is as much a cross-dresser as Viola, but what he crosses is a boundary of rank rather than of gender. (1993, 36)

Malvolio doesn't actually wear this embroidered velvet gown, so he isn't actually a cross-dresser, but he *would* be if he could. We must recognize, however, that Malvolio's fantasy reflects, among other things, an attack on the status quo. Malvolio can be seen as a person who wishes to rise in the world and fantasizes about what his life would be like were he to do so. Therefore, beneath the laughter and ridicule, an element of status anxiety is found in this scene. Malvolio is so delusional that he thinks Olivia dotes on him and that he will be able to marry her.

Discrepant Awareness and Comedy

In this scene a person talks about and insults others who, without his being aware of it, are spying on him and listening to him speak. They, in turn, insult him, as his fantasy progresses. Here, the techniques of revelation and insult play an important role along with ignorance or discrepant awareness. There are three levels of this discrepant awareness: the audience is observing Maria and Sir Toby and their colleagues who are, in turn, hiding from and observing Malvolio. (Garber suggests there is also a subtle hint of a masturbatory fantasy, as Malvolio talks about "playing with my—some rich jewel." He interrupts himself to substitute something conventionally acceptable, but there is reason to suspect that masturbation is what is really on his mind.)

There are other examples of discrepant awareness to be considered, besides that of Malvolio, who mistakes Maria's letter for one from Olivia. Orsino, for example, is not aware that Cesario is really a woman, Viola. And neither is Olivia, who falls in love with Cesario. Antonio, Sebastian's friend, becomes confused when he thinks he is talking to Sebastian but is really talking with Cesario, who doesn't know what Antonio is talking about when he asks for his money. And Olivia mistakes Sebastian for Cesario and gets married, discovering only later that she has married Viola's identical twin brother. In addition, Sir Toby and Sir Andrew, thinking they were fighting the "feminine" Cesario actually picked a fight with Sebastian, and got a bloody beating for their pains. Thus, a great deal of the humor in the play stems from a lack of awareness on the part of the characters about the identity of Cesario and of Malvolio's mistake regarding the letter. It is to this letter that we now turn.

The Trout that was Caught with Tickling

After she drops her letter in Malvolio's path, Maria says that Malvolio's a "trout that must be caught with tickling." After Malvolio's fantasy about becoming a Count is revealed, he walks along and discovers the letter Maria has left for him.

> MALVOLIO: By my life, this my lady's hand. These be her very C's, her U's, and her T's; and thus makes she her great P's. It is, in contempt of question, her hand.
>
> (Act 2, scene 5)

Shakespeare is being a bit bawdy here, spelling out the word "cunt," from which she "pees." Lest we miss the joke, Shakespeare has Sir Andrew repeat things for us.

SIR ANDREW: Her C's, her U's and her T's. Why that?

Malvolio then reads part of the letter, addressed to "an unknown beloved" and sealed with Olivia's seal. I will skip part of the letter here, to pinpoint the most interesting sections. Malvolio reads a poem that is very meaningful to him.

MALVOLIO: "I may command where I adore
But silence, like a Lucrece knife,
With bloodless stroke my heart doth gore.
M, O, A, I, doth sway my life."

He then deconstructs the letter.

MALVOLIO: "I may command where I adore." Why, she may command me. I serve her, she is my lady. Why, this is evident to any formal capacity, there is no obstruction in this.

He notices a prose section that he reads aloud:

MALVOLIO: If this fall into thy hand, revolve. In my stars I am above thee; but be not afraid of greatness. Some are born great, some achieve greatness, and some have greatness thrust upon 'em. Thy Fates open their hands. Let thy blood and spirit embrace them, and to inure thyself to what thou art like to be, cast thy humble slough and appear fresh. Be opposite with a kinsman, surly with servants, let thy tongue tang arguments of state, put thyself into the trick of singularity. She thus advises thee that sighs for thee. Remember who commended thy yellow stockings and wished to see thee ever cross-gartered. I say, remember. Go to, thou art made, if thou desirest to be so. If not, let me see thee a steward still, the fellow of servants, and not worthy to touch Fortune's fingers. Farewell. She that would alter services with thee,

THE FORTUNATE UNHAPPY

(Act 2, scene 5)

Finally he reads the postscript:

MALVOLIO: Thou canst not choose but know who I am. If thou entertainest my love, let it appear in thy smiling. Thy smiles become thee well, therefore in my presence still smile, dear my sweet, I prithee."

(Act 2, scene 5)

Malvolio doesn't recognize that he is being made the victim of a practical joke, and assumes the letter is from Olivia. Sir Toby comments that he finds the joke so delightful that he could marry Maria for being clever enough to think it up. He also wonders, showing a touch of humanity, whether this joke will have serious consequences for Malvolio.

> SIR TOBY: Why, thou hast put him in such a dream that when the image of it leaves him he must run mad.
>
> (Act 2, scene 5)

Maria replies "Nay, but say true." She asks whether he has fallen for the trick and is told that he has. She then explains to Sir Toby, Sir Andrew and Fabian that the instructions in the letter are designed to make Olivia despise Malvolio, for it turns out that she abhors the color yellow, detests cross-gartering, and being in mourning for her brother, will find Malvolio's constant smiling contemptible.

Two scenes later, we find ourselves back in Olivia's garden. In a scene that, when performed well, is screamingly funny, Olivia asks Maria where Malvolio is, and she plants the notion in Olivia's mind that Malvolio is crazy.

> MARIA: He's coming, madam, but in very strange manner. He is sure possessed, madam.
>
> OLIVIA: Why, what's the matter? Does he rave?
>
> MARIA: No, madam, he does nothing but smile. Your ladyship were best to have some guard about you if he come, for sure the man is tainted in his wits.
>
> (Act 3, scene 4)

When Malvolio appears, he assumes that Olivia has sent him the letter and makes allusions to it, but she does not know what he is talking about. Malvolio misinterprets everything Olivia says and Olivia thinks that he is mad.

Olivia sends Maria to fetch Malvolio, and when he appears, Olivia asks him "How now, Malvolio?"

> MALVOLIO: Sweet lady, ho, ho.
>
> OLIVIA: Smilest thou?
> I sent for thee upon a sad occasion.
>
> MALVOLIO: Sad, lady? I could be sad. This does make some obstruction in the blood, this cross-gartering, but what of that? If it please the eye of one, it is with me as the very true sonnet is, "Please one, and please all."
>
> (Act 3, scene 4)

Olivia is confused and asks Malvolio what's the matter with him. He replies, making further allusions to the letter, about wearing yellow stockings and saying that he recognizes her sweet Roman hand in the letter she sent him.

Thinking he is sick, Olivia asks him whether he is going to go to bed, since he is acting in such a bizarre manner and seems to be crazy. Malvolio misunderstands her question, interpreting it in the light of the letter he has received that he believes, mistakenly, was from her. Let us look at the way the dialogue develops.

> OLIVIA: Wilt thou go to bed, Malvolio?
> MALVOLIO: To bed! Aye, sweetheart, and I'll come to thee.
> OLIVIA: God comfort thee! Why doest thou smile so and kiss thy hand so oft?
> MARIA: How do you, Malvolio?
> MALVOLIO: At your request! Yes, nightingales answer daws.
> MARIA: Why appear you with this ridiculous boldness before my lady?
> MALVOLIO: "Be not afraid of greatness." T'was well writ.
> OLIVIA: What meanest thou by that, Malvolio?
> MALVOLIO: "Some are born great—"
> OLIVIA: Ha!
> MALVOLIO: "Some achieve greatness—"
> OLIVIA: What sayest thou?
> MALVOLIO: "And some have greatness thrust upon them."
> OLIVIA: Heaven restore thee.
>
> (Act 3, scene 4)

Malvolio continues to babble on about the yellow stockings and dressing in a cross-gartered manner, leading Olivia finally to conclude he is suffering from a "midsummer madness." When a servant announces that Cesario is waiting to see her, she leaves, telling Maria to have Malvolio taken care of. There is, we should note, a tone of affection in her words; Olivia does not wish any harm to come to Malvolio and seems afraid he might do something injurious to himself.

> OLIVIA: Good Maria, let this fellow be looked to. Where's my cousin Toby? Let some of my people have a special care of him. I would not have him miscarry for the half of my dowry.
>
> (Act 3, scene 4)

Malvolio completely misinterprets everything and puts a positive construction on Olivia's words. He believes that she is sending Toby to look after him so Malvolio can be "opposite" with him, and he makes much of the fact that Olivia said "let this fellow" rather than something like "Malvolio, my steward." This confirms his belief that the letter is genuine and everything is working out as planned, and his fortune is assured.

> MALVOLIO: "Let this fellow be looked to." Fellow! Not Malvolio, after my degree, but fellow. Why, everything adheres together, that no dram of a scruple, no scruple of a scruple, no obstacle, no incredulous or unsafe circumstance—What can be said? Nothing that can be can come between me and the full prospect of my hopes.
>
> (Act 3, scene 4)

When Maria brings Sir Toby and Fabian to talk with Malvolio, he tells them to go hang themselves, says that they are shallow and not of his element, and leaves. They decide to carry out the joke (especially since Olivia believes Malvolio is undergoing a bout of midsummer's madness) until they get bored—and when they do, they will reveal the truth.

Shakespeare is using Malvolio to focus attention on human obstinacy, blindness, and stupidity—ridiculing the tendency people have to construe events to suit their purposes and preconceptions, regardless of what is actually occurring. Malvolio is unaware that he is the victim of a practical joke, and thus misconstrues Olivia's words, by a process of selective attention, so that they will support his fantasies.

At the end of the play, Maria, Sir Toby, and Fabian are bored with their joke, afraid that when the joke is revealed it will have serious consequences, and unsure how to put an end to things. The joke is revealed when Malvolio sends a letter from his dungeon to Olivia and attaches the letter that Maria wrote to him. Olivia recognizes immediately that it has been forged by Maria. She sends for Malvolio, explains to him that it was not she, but Maria, who wrote the letter he found, and says that he will have the opportunity to decide how Maria and her colleagues will be punished. Fabian confesses:

> FABIAN: Most freely I confess, myself and Toby
> Set this device against Malvolio here,
> Upon some stubborn and uncourteous parts
> We had conceived against him. Maria writ
> The letter at Sir Toby's great importance,
> In recompense whereof he hath married her.
> How with a sportful malice it was followed
> May rather pluck on laughter than revenge,

> If that the injuries be justly weighed
> That have on both sides passed.
>
> (Act 5, scene 1)

Malvolio's last lines in the play are "I'll be revenged on the whole pack of you." He then exits. The following dialogue occurs:

> OLIVIA: He hath been most notoriously abused.
> DUKE: Pursue him, and entreat him to a peace.
>
> (Act 5, scene 1)

The resolution of the matter is not really dealt with, but merely suggested. Fabian has argued that he, Sir Toby, and Maria decided to play their practical joke on Malvolio because he had been hostile to them, and suggests that everyone should focus on the humor in the "device" rather than the injury it caused.

Shakespeare is pointing out here that practical jokes often cause a great deal of suffering and injury and that people who make such jokes are usually very hostile, if not sadistic. Sometimes the perpetrators of these jokes find themselves in unanticipated situations from which they have difficulty extricating themselves. They often end up suffering themselves.

The ridicule directed at Malvolio, I have suggested, has a political dimension to it also, for Malvolio was a person who dreamed of moving up in the world, a steward who dreamed of becoming a Count—in ridiculing him Shakespeare was directing laughter at others like him, who entertained the same hopes and aspirations. Thus we can see the joke on Malvolio as being "instructive" to those who might want to attack the status quo. It is also a means of reinforcing the notion that the prevailing arrangement of classes was correct and reasonable.

Malvolio is not the only ridiculous figure in the play. Most of the characters, both high and low, are driven by passions and have a comic dimension to them. Orsino is obsessed with his love for Olivia; Olivia is overcome with sadness over the death of her brother (though she forgets about it immediately when she falls in love with Cesario); Sir Toby Belch is a drunkard; Sir Andrew Aguecheek is an argumentative and spendthrift fool—and a coward, to boot. Viola is, in a sense, a victim of her disguise as she cannot declare her love for Orsino. Only Maria, a variant of the shrewd servant figure that we saw in *Miles Gloriosus*, and Feste, the professional fool, seem to be balanced and normal. Comedy is, we must remember, about various bizarre and eccentric types who find themselves in some kind of mess and have to figure out how to get out of it. The traditional ending of a romantic comedy is a marriage, and in *Twelfth Night* we have three: Sir Toby marries Maria, Olivia marries Sebastian, and Viola marries Orsino.

In *Shakespeare and the Ends of Comedy*, Ejner J. Jensen argues that in *Twelfth Night* Shakespeare was more interested in "short term effects over comprehensive design" (1991, 100) and that we should see the play as more a series of independent comic events rather than as being a coherent whole. Jensen's book attacks the focus on endings in Shakespeare's comedies—a theme, he suggests, that is found in the critical writings of Northrop Frye and C. L. Barber. This dominant critical tradition has, Jensen argues, focused too much attention on closure, led to teleological criticism, and neglected the richness of the plays. He writes:

> Thus, closure in *Twelfth Night*, far from being the key to interpretation and far from being problematic, is a dramatically skillful realization of connections prepared for and pre-enacted in the play's earlier events. It provides satisfaction not because it answers questions but because it presents the promised answers in such dramatically satisfying ways. (1991, 117)

The conclusion of *Twelfth Night* is, it would seem, almost an afterthought, as Shakespeare ties all the loose knots and unties all the difficult ones in a very short time. His focus was, it might be said, on the courtships rather than the marriages. (Like a fairy tale, a complicated story ends with the moral equivalent of "...then they got married and everyone lived happily ever after.") We must keep in mind, here, that Malvolio, like Orsino and Sir Andrew Aguecheek, sees himself as Olivia's suitor; unfortunately his suit is as hopeless as theirs. In *Twelfth Night* Shakespeare has created a remarkable collection of comic individuals (and individuals who are made comic) and used various techniques of humor with unparalleled brilliance. It is a work that remains hilarious and amuses and speaks to people—about everything from the nature of love and illusion to the question of gender identity—almost four hundred years after it was written.

4

No Trusting to Appearances: *The School for Scandal*

Richard Brinsley Sheridan's *The School for Scandal* was first performed at the Drury Lane Theatre in 1777 and was, for many years, one of the most popular comedies in the English language. Early in the first act the elements of the plot are revealed.

The Plot

Lady Sneerwell loves Charles Surface, who has the reputation of being an extravagant libertine. He is in love with and is loved by Maria, who is the object of affection (more for her money than anything else) of Joseph Surface, Charles's brother, who pretends to be prudent and benevolent, but is really just the opposite. Joseph has entered into an alliance with Lady Sneerwell to break up Charles and Maria's relationship. Charles and Joseph Surface are both wards of Sir Peter Teazle, a man in his fifties who has just married for the first time. His wife is a young woman, Lady Teazle, who has become a gossip and a spendthrift. Sir Peter wants Maria to leave Charles and give her heart to Joseph, but she loathes him. Joseph, in turn, is involved in a would-be affair with Lady Teazle, who does not know Joseph wishes to marry Maria.

The alliance between Joseph Surface and Lady Sneerwell is revealed shortly after Lady Sneerwell has been introduced. Lady Sneerwell is talking with Snake, who has just forged part of a letter that will be used to cause mischief, which suggests that Charles is involved with Lady Sneerwell. She is discussing Joseph Surface.

> SNEERWELL: His real attachment is to Maria or her fortune; but, finding his brother a favoured rival, he has been obliged to mask his pretensions, and profit by my assistance.

SNAKE: Yet still I am more puzzled why you should interest yourself in his success.

SNEERWELL: Heavens! how dull you are! Cannot you surmise the weakness which I hitherto, through shame, have concealed even from you? Must I confess that Charles—that libertine, that extravagant, that bankrupt in fortune and reputation—that he it is for whom I am anxious and malicious, and to gain whom I would sacrifice everything?

SNAKE: Now, indeed, your conduct appears consistent; but how came you and Mr. Surface so confidential?

SNEERWELL: For our mutual interest. I have found him out a long time since. I know him to be artful, selfish, and malicious—in short, a sentimental knave; while with Sir Peter, and indeed with all his acquaintance, he passes for a youthful miracle of prudence, good sense, and benevolence.

SNAKE: Yes: yet Sir Peter vows he has not his equal in England; and, above all, he praises him as a man of sentiment.

(Act 1, scene 1)

In the first minutes of the play, then, we find a complicated situation in which what I would describe as comedic tension is created. That is, we have conflicting desires among characters who have a variety of motivations. Lady Sneerwell hopes to steal Charles from Maria and thus will help Joseph Surface steal Maria (and her fortune) from Charles. Will they be able to do this? If so, how? We also find that Joseph Surface is an *eiron* figure, a pretender, and this generates some additional tension: will he be found out and punished, or will he be able to dupe everyone (except for Lady Sneerwell, that is)?

Names of Characters

Most of the characters in the play have names that reveal something about them. As Harry Levin writes in *Playboys & Killjoys*, "Comedy has habitually set great store by onomastics, the science of naming, and by what the Germans call *redended namen*, speaking names. In English we may call them charactonyms, names that describe the characters" (1987, 73).

Thus we have characters named Careless, Snake, Bumper, Sneerwell, Candour, and Backbite whose personalities are more or less self-evident. Sir Peter Teazle is a bit more complicated. The term "teazel" is a variant of *teasel*, a plant with prickly leaves or burrs. The name Surface is used somewhat ironically, for what is important about Charles and Joseph is what is hidden, though in Joseph's case, most people are taken in by what appears on the surface.

We have a pretty good idea from the names of these characters what they will be like and we are not disappointed. Most of the characters are scandal mongers who delight, for a variety of reasons, in spreading malicious gossip about people. Lady Sneerwell confesses her reason to Snake.

> SNEERWELL: ...Wounded myself, in the early part of my life, by the envenomed tongue of slander, I confess I have since known no pleasure equal to the reducing others to the level of my own injured reputation.
>
> (Act 1, scene 1)

She has been victimized and gains pleasure in victimizing others. Gossip and scandal mongering are based on allusions—references to bad things people have done, exposures of sexual misconduct and so forth. There is a wonderful scene involving Mrs. Candour and Joseph Surface. Maria suggests that gossips are equally culpable as the people being gossiped about. Mrs. Candour replies as follows.

> CANDOUR: To be sure they are: tale-bearers are as bad as the tale-makers—'tis an old observation, and a very true one: but what's to be done, as I said before?... To-day, Mrs. Clackitt assured me, Mr. and Mrs. Honeymoon were at last become mere man and wife, like the rest of their acquaintance. She likewise hinted that a certain widow, in the next street, had got rid of her dropsy and recovered her shape in a most surprising manner. And at the same time Miss Tattle, who was by, affirmed, that Lord Buffalo had discovered his lady at a house of no extraordinary fame; and that Sir Harry Bouquet and Tom Saunter were to measure swords on a similar provocation. But, Lord, do you think I would report these things! No, no! tale-bearers, as I said before, are just as bad as the tale-makers.
>
> JOSEPH: Ah! Mrs. Candour, if everybody had your forbearance and good nature!
>
> CANDOUR: I confess, Mr. Surface, I cannot bear to hear people attacked behind their backs; and when ugly circumstances come out against our acquaintance I own I always love to think the best. By-the-by, I hope 'tis not true that your brother is absolutely ruined?
>
> (Act 1, scene 1)

What we have here is Mrs. Candour telling us she doesn't believe in gossip or tale-telling while, at the same time, she slanders a number of different people. *Candor* means being open and sincere, and Mrs. Candour is just the opposite of that, contradicting herself as she speaks and revealing herself as a hypocrite.

On Mistakes Made by Gossipers and Their Use of Insult

The conversation then turns to gossip about a number of other people. One of the characters, Crabtree, reports about a party he attended in which the conversation turned to sheep breeding. A deaf dowager, Lady Dowager Dundizzy, mistakes what someone says about a Miss Piper's goat having twins, for Miss Piper having twins. "The mistake, as you may imagine, threw the whole company into a fit of laughter," Crabtree reports. But by the next morning gossipers spread the rumor that Miss Piper gave birth to twins, a boy and a girl. Others decide who the father was and proclaim that they know the farmhouse where the twins were sent to nurse.

Sheridan is satirizing the way gossip spreads and takes on a life of its own, inventing more and more preposterous details as different gossipers embellish the original story and invent new details. In addition to the fantastic imaginations of the gossipers, there is also a good deal of aggression and hostility. For example, in one scene a number of the characters are talking about a woman, Miss Vermillion.

> LADY SNEERWELL: Oh, surely she is a pretty woman.
>
> CRABTREE: I am very glad you think so, ma'am.
>
> MRS. CANDOUR: She has a charming fresh colour.
>
> LADY TEAZLE: Yes, when it is fresh put on.
>
> MRS. CANDOUR: Oh, fie! I'll swear her colour is natural: I have seen it come and go!
>
> LADY TEAZLE: I dare swear you have, ma'am. it goes off at night, and comes again in the morning.
>
> SIR BENJAMIN: True, ma'am, it not only comes and goes; but, what's more, egad, her maid can fetch and carry it!
>
> (Act 2, scene 2)

Later, the discussion turns to Mrs. Candour's cousin, Ogle, who has "pretensions...to be critical on beauty."

> CRABTREE: Oh, to be sure! she has herself the oddest countenance that ever was seen; 'tis a collection of features from all the different countries of the globe.
>
> SIR BENJAMIN: So she has, indeed—an Irish front—
>
> CRABTREE: Caledonian locks—
>
> SIR BENJAMIN: Dutch nose—

CRABTREE:	Austrian lips—
SIR BENJAMIN:	Complexion of a Spaniard—
CRABTREE:	And teeth *à la Chinoise*—
SIR BENJAMIN:	In short, her face resembles a *table d'hôte* at Spa—where no two guests are of a nation.
CRABTREE:	Or a congress at the close of a general war—wherein all the members, even to her eyes, appear to have a different interest, and her nose and her chin are the only parties likely to join issue.

(Act 2, scene 2)

This dialogue is full of insults about Miss Ogle, a person the insulters dine with twice a week, as it turns out. Insults by themselves, as I have suggested earlier, are not humorous. But in the frame of reference in which they are found, a dramatic comedy peopled by characters who are ridiculous comic types—gossips and slanderers—the aggression found in the insults is tempered. Sir Benjamin Backbite and Crabtree engage in a catalogue of insults, ending with the suggestion that poor Miss Ogle's nose and chin are joined.

The gossips and slanderers are unable to control themselves and abstain from saying nasty things about people they know, alluding to embarrassing aspects of the behavior of their friends and enemies for instance. They are comic types who, with every insult or bit of gossip, make themselves more comic and more the objects of our laughter. Thus we get a double playoff from these characters: we participate in their humorous aggression (even though we feel judgmental about it) and we laugh at these characters, who reveal themselves to be eccentric comic types.

Old Husbands and Young Wives

Sir Peter Teazle and his wife spend a good deal of time bickering. She tells him that though she was educated in the country, she has learned that after marriage women of fashion in London "are accountable to nobody." He replies that he won't be ruined by her extravagances. An amusing bit of dialogue follows.

LADY TEAZLE:	For my part, I should think you would like to have your wife thought a woman of taste.
SIR PETER:	Ay—there again—taste. Zounds! madam you had no taste when you married me!

(Act 2, scene 1)

This is a good example of how dialogue can be used to create humor. I would classify this as an example of the technique of wordplay—based on the ambiguity of words, and language in general. When Sir Peter says his wife had no taste when he married her, he means she hadn't become a fancy lady concerned about fashion when he married her. But what he says is that she had no taste (that is, poor taste) when she married *him*. Inadvertently, he has insulted himself and made himself somewhat ridiculous.

In a later scene, Sir Peter and his wife decide to make up and "never differ again." But this is followed, shortly, by more fighting that starts when they disagree about who starts their fights.

SIR PETER: ...'tis evident you never cared a pin for me, and I was a madman to marry you—a pert, rural coquette, that had refused half the honest 'squires in the neighbourhood!

LADY TEAZLE: And I am sure I was a fool to marry you—an old dangling bachelor, who was single at fifty, only because he never could meet with any one who would have him.

(Act 3, scene 1)

Sir Peter then says that he now believes the reports he's heard about her having a relationship with Charles to be true and she denies it. They then agree to separate, at which point she says that the two of them "are of a mind once more."

The plot is further complicated because Joseph Surface has become involved in a love affair with Lady Teazle.

JOSEPH: A curious dilemma, truly, my politics have run me into! I wanted, at first, only to ingratiate myself with Lady Teazle, that she might not be my enemy with Maria; and I have, I don't know how, become her serious lover. Sincerely I begin to wish I had never made such a point of gaining so very good a character, for it has led me into so many cursed rogueries that I doubt I shall be exposed at last.

(Act 2, scene 2)

It is, in fact, this relationship that will lead to his downfall, when Lady Teazle is discovered hiding behind a screen in his apartment.

A Further Complication: Sir Oliver Surface Surfaces

At this point another complication in the plot occurs. Sir Oliver Surface, the wealthy uncle of Charles and Joseph, has returned, earlier than

No Trusting to Appearances: *The School for Scandal* 89

expected, from abroad. He is told about the reputations of the two brothers and decides to see for himself what they are like. Rowley, a friend, suggests a scheme by which he could find out what they are like, by impersonating a certain Mr. Stanley, a merchant who was ruined by undeserved misfortunes. Charles has sent money to the man and Joseph has not, giving only evasive promises of future help.

At this point, a character named Moses, a "friendly Jew" is mentioned, as waiting to see them. He has, Rowley tells Sir Oliver, "done everything in his power to bring your nephew to a proper sense of his extravagance." Moses is then brought in and talks about his dealings with Charles. He mentions that he had agreed to bring a moneylender Charles had never met to him, a certain Mr. Premium. Sir Peter suggests that Sir Oliver pretend to be Premium, rather than Stanley, and so the plot switches once again.

When Moses and Sir Oliver, impersonating Mr. Premium, get together with Charles, he offers a disquisition on his character.

CHARLES: I am an extravagant young fellow who wants to borrow money; you I take to be a prudent old fellow, who has got money to lend. I am a blockhead enough to give fifty per cent sooner than not have it! and you, I presume, are rogue enough to take a hundred if you can get it.

(Act 3, scene 3)

Sir Oliver, pretending to be Premium, says he doesn't have money but knows someone who does have money, but wants something in return. Surface remarks that he has important connections and tells him about his rich uncle.

CHARLES: Then you must know that I have a devilish rich uncle in the East Indies, Sir Oliver Surface, from whom I have the greatest expectations.
SIR OLIVER: That you have a wealthy uncle, I have heard; but how your expectations will turn out is more, I believe, than you can tell.
CHARLES: Oh, no!—there can be no doubt. They tell me I'm a prodigious favourite, and that he talks of leaving me everything.
SIR OLIVER: Indeed! this is the first I've heard of it.

(Act 3, scene 3)

He then asks Charles whether he has anything he could dispose of, to serve as collateral. Charles tells him that all he has left are some old paintings and that he'll auction them off for some money, with his friend,

Careless, acting as auctioneer. Charles notices that Premium doesn't "seem to like the business."

> SIR OLIVER: Oh, yes, I do, vastly! Ha! ha! ha! yes, yes, I think it a rare joke to sell one's family by auction—ha! ha!—[*Aside*] Oh, the prodigal!

They then go to the picture room in Charles's house and start auctioning off the paintings. He starts auctioning off the paintings, and eventually they get to an early portrait of Sir Oliver, done before he went to India.

> CARELESS: Your uncle Oliver! God, then you'll never be friends, Charles. That, now, to me, is as stern a looking rogue as ever I saw; an unforgiving eye, and a damned disinheriting countenance! an inveterate knave, depend on't. Don't you think so, little Premium?
>
> SIR OLIVER: Upon my soul, sir, I do not; I think it is as honest a face as any in the room, dead or alive. But I suppose uncle Oliver goes with the rest of the lumber?
>
> CHARLES: No, hang it! I'll not part with poor Noll. The old fellow has been very good to me, and, egad, I'll keep his picture while I've a room to put it in.

Sir Oliver then tries to pry the picture away by offering eight hundred pounds to Charles, but he refuses to give the painting up. Sir Oliver then gives him the eight hundred pounds, saying he'll settle on the details with him later, and then leaves with Moses. Charles gives Rowley one hundred pounds to bring to Stanley. Rowley leaves and tells Sir Oliver about the money that Charles has sent to Stanley.

A Comic Denouement

The comic denouement of the play occurs in a scene in which Lady Teazle has come to visit Joseph Surface. She tells him that her husband has become very jealous of her and thinks she is having an affair with Charles. Joseph, whose friends have spread the rumor, offers the following advice.

> JOSEPH: When a husband entertains a groundless suspicion of his wife, and withdraws his confidence from her, the original compact is broken, and she owes it to the honour of her sex to endeavor to outwit him.
>
> (Act 4, scene 3)

He adds that it is her consciousness of her innocence that is causing the problem and that she is "like a person in a plethora, absolutely dying from too much health."

> LADY TEAZLE: So, so; then I perceive your prescription is, that I must sin in my own defence, and part with my virtue to preserve my reputation?
> JOSEPH: Exactly so, upon my credit ma'am.
> LADY TEAZLE: Well, certainly this is the oddest doctrine, and the newest receipt for avoiding calumny?
>
> (Act 4, scene 3)

Joseph takes her hand, to begin seducing her, when they are interrupted by a servant informing them that Sir Peter has appeared and will be in the room shortly. Lady Teazle screams that she is ruined. "What will become of me? Now, Mr. Logic..." She hears Sir Peter on the stairs and runs and hides behind a screen in Joseph's room. Joseph grabs a book and pretends to be reading. Sir Peter enters, finds Joseph reading a book, and comments that he is always "improving" himself.

He has come, he tells Joseph, because Lady Teazle's conduct has made him very unhappy. He had good authority, he adds, to believe that she has formed an attachment to someone else...namely, Charles.

> JOSEPH: My brother! impossible!
> SIR PETER: Oh, my dear friend, the goodness of your own heart misleads you. You judge of others by yourself.
> JOSEPH: Certainly, Sir Peter, the heart that is conscious of its own integrity is ever slow to credit another's treachery.
>
> (Act 3, scene 3)

They discuss Sir Peter's problems with his wife and the treachery of Charles. Joseph pretends to be sympathetic.

> JOSEPH: However, if it should be proved on him, he is no longer a brother of mine—I disclaim kindred with him: for the man who break the laws of hospitality, and tempt the wife of his friend, deserves to be branded as the pest of society.
>
> (Act 3, scene 3)

Sir Peter says he has drafts of two deeds relating to his giving or leaving money to his wife and asks Joseph which he thinks is the best arrangement. Then Sir Peter asks Joseph how he is doing in his courting of Maria and his attempts to steal her away from Charles.

SIR PETER:	And now, my dear friend, if you please, we will talk of the situation of your hopes with Maria.
JOSEPH:	[*Softly.*] Oh, no, Sir Peter; another time, if you please.
SIR PETER:	I am sensibly chagrined at the little progress you seem to make in her affections.
JOSEPH:	[*Softly.*] I beg you will not mention it. What are my disappointments when your happiness is in debate! [*Aside.*] 'Sdeath, I shall be ruined every way!

(Act 3, scene 3)

At this moment, the servant runs in to say that Charles is coming. Sir Peter tells Joseph to ask him about his relationship with Lady Teazle while he hides in the closet. Just before he runs into the closet he notices a petticoat, but Joseph tells him it is that of a little French milliner who plagues him. What follows then is a fine example of farce, in which characters keep popping in and out of hiding.

LADY TEAZLE:	[*Peeping.*] Couldn't I steal off?
JOSEPH:	Keep close, my angel!
SIR PETER:	[*Peeping.*] Joseph, tax him home.
JOSEPH:	Back, my dear friend!
LADY TEAZLE:	[*Peeping.*] Couldn't you lock Sir Peter in?
JOSEPH:	Be still, my life.
SIR PETER:	[*Peeping.*] You're sure the milliner won't blab?
JOSEPH:	In, in, my dear Sir Peter!—'Fore Gad, I wish I had a key to the door.

(Act 3, scene 3)

Charles appears and Joseph tries to get him to inadvertently confess to liking Lady Teazle; Charles replies that the idea is foolish, especially since everyone knows that he loves Maria. Charles then says he always thought that Joseph was her favorite, and mentions finding them together in Joseph's chambers a number of times. Joseph pulls him aside and tells him that Sir Peter is in the closet, and has overheard everything they've said. At this, Charles pulls Sir Peter out of the closet. He tells Charles not to be angry with Joseph, who acted under Sir Peter's direction.

Just then, the servant appears again and informs them that Lady Sneerwell has arrived. He decides to intercept her below and leaves, reminding Sir Peter not to say anything about the French milliner. After he leaves, Charles says that Joseph is "too moral by half." Sir Peter replies that Joseph isn't as innocent as he seems and mentions that there's a French milliner hiding behind the screen. At this, Charles throws down the screen, revealing Lady Teazle.

Joseph returns and finds that Lady Teazle has been discovered. He concocts a story about her visiting him in order to help him obtain Maria's favors. Sir Peter accepts this, but when he asks his wife to verify the story, she reveals that Joseph is a scoundrel and a hypocrite.

> LADY TEAZLE: Hear me, Sir Peter! I came here on no matter relating to your ward, and even ignorant of this gentleman's pretensions to her. But I came, seduced by his insidious arguments, at least to listen to his pretended passion, if not to sacrifice your honour to his baseness.
>
> (Act 3, scene 3)

She adds that she has been touched by Sir Peter's tenderness toward her, has recovered her senses, and will no longer to listen to the "smooth-tongued hypocrite" Joseph.

On Sheridan's Comic Devices

In these last scenes, Sheridan uses a number of comic devices brilliantly. First, he uses the technique of impersonation and has Sir Oliver impersonate Mr. Premium. This leads to the wonderful scene in which Charles says he has a rich uncle who favors him and of whom he has the greatest expectations. Sir Oliver, as Mr. Premium, says he's heard of the rich uncle, but not that he favors Charles. "This is the first I've heard of it," he says. Later, when the auction begins and Careless is shown an early portrait of Sir Oliver, he says a number of insulting things about him, calling him a "rogue" and a "knave."

In these scenes, we not only have impersonation but also ignorance. It is not the revelation of ignorance but the opposite—characters are put in a situation in which they are made ignorant, so to speak, by the impersonation. The humor is intensified when the characters talk about and insult Sir Oliver, not knowing that the person they are talking to is actually Sir Oliver.

We find a variation of this technique during the scene in Joseph Surface's apartment, when characters talk about people who are hidden that overhear what is said. That scene also involves embarrassment and the attempt to escape from it, and exposure, as Joseph hides Lady Teazle behind a screen and Sir Peter Teazle in a closet, hoping he can keep them unaware of one another's presence. There is also the matter of coincidence. Joseph is unfortunate, as one character after another converges on his apartment, revealing things that Joseph wants to keep hidden—such as his desire to marry Maria, which Lady Teazle knows nothing about.

Also, when Joseph's treachery is discovered, we have the technique of unmasking, which is generally tied to pretense. Joseph has pretended to be a fine, upstanding, serious person but is unmasked as a hypocritical rogue. He has, actually, outwitted himself by trying to juggle too many balls at the same time. He is involved in so many intrigues that eventually he trips himself up.

A Final Impersonation

Sir Oliver next impersonates Stanley and visits Joseph, to see what he is like. Joseph offers platitudes but refuses to help him. Sir Oliver, as Stanley, remarks that if Sir Oliver were around, he would be of help and that he thinks that Sir Oliver's bounty will enable Joseph to be charitable. He replies that Stanley is misinformed about Sir Oliver, who really is avaricious.

> JOSEPH: My dear sir, you were strangely misinformed. Sir Oliver is a worthy man, a very worthy man; but avarice, Mr. Stanley, is the vice of age. I will tell you, my good sir, in confidence, what he has done for me has been a mere nothing; though people, I know, have thought otherwise, and, for my part, I never chose to contradict the report.
> SIR OLIVER: What! has he never transmitted you bullion—rupees—pagodas?
> JOSEPH: Oh, dear sir, nothing of the kind! No, no; a few presents now and then—china, shawls, congou tea, avadavats, and Indian crackers—little more, believe me.
>
> (Act 5, scene 1)

Joseph adds that he has lent his brother a great deal of money. With that, Joseph calls his servants, and after the two men exchange civilities in an exaggerated manner, Sir Oliver leaves, with an aside to the effect that Joseph is a "dissembler."

Sheridan further satirizes gossipers with a scene in which different stories about what happened in Joseph Surface's apartment are making the rounds—namely that there was a duel between Sir Peter and Joseph Surface. Sir Benjamin Backbite holds that the duelers used swords; Mr. Crabtree insists that they used pistols, and that Sir Peter is gravely ill, with a bullet in his thorax. Everything is finally resolved when Sir Peter appears, alive and well. A final plot by Joseph Surface, based on a forged letter linking Charles Surface and Lady Teazle, is thwarted when Rowland explains that the letter is a forgery. He has learned this from Snake, who remarks to Lady Sneerwell, "you paid me extremely liberally for the lie in question; but I unfortunately have been offered double to speak the truth."

SNEERWELL: The torments of shame and disappointment on you all! [*Going.*]

LADY TEAZLE: Hold, Lady Sneerwell—before you go, let me thank you for the trouble you and that gentleman have taken in writing letters from me to Charles, and answering them yourself; and let me also request you to make my respects to the scandalous college, of which you are president, and inform them, that Lady Teazle, licentiate, begs to return the diploma they granted her, as she leaves off practice and kills characters no longer.

(Act 5, scene 3)

Conclusions

The play ends with Sir Peter and his wife reconciled, the gossipers thrown out of his house, and Charles and Maria reunited and set to be married the next day. But the play is not so much about gossip and scandal as is it about reality and illusion, deception and the uncovering of deception. There are two characters who deceive others: Joseph Surface and Sir Oliver Surface. Joseph is a villainous deceiver, who allies himself with Lady Sneerwell and seeks, by forging letters and other ploys, to steal Maria (and her fortune) away from his brother Charles. Sir Oliver is a beneficent deceiver, who impersonates Mr. Premium and Mr. Stanley, to ascertan for himself what his nephews are really like.

While impersonating these two characters, Sir Oliver finds himself in situations in which different characters (such as Charles, Careless, and Joseph) tell him about Sir Oliver, sometimes describing Sir Oliver in most unflattering terms. The technique used here is ignorance, as characters, not realizing they are talking to Sir Oliver, talk about him. Audiences find this kind of humor delicious, since they identify with the character doing the impersonating and can relish the ways in which the characters make fools of themselves.

Joseph Surface, on the other hand, is a rascal and trickster figure, who ultimately outsmarts himself. He is an *eiron* or dissembler, who successfully fools people about his "good character" until his luck changes and, as a result of coincidence—unexpected visits by Sir Peter and Charles—Lady Teazle and Sir Oliver discover what Joseph has been up to and what a rogue he really is.

The play also deals with scandal, and can be looked upon as a sociological study of rumor—the way people embellish the truth and fabricate all kinds of stories as information passes from person to person. Sheridan satirizes these people, heaping ridicule on them and their foolish pretensions. Scandal involves the matter of illusion and reality, just like deception—though scandal is indirect and based on hearsay. The backbone of the play then, involves the opposition between illusion and reality, deception versus truthfulness, impersonation versus recognition. Lady Teazle may resign from the college of scandal mongers, but all who read or see *The School for Scandal* learn a great deal about many other subjects.

5

The Devices of Absurdity: *The Bald Soprano*

Ionesco's "anti-play", *The Bald Soprano*, is one of the most celebrated and interesting works in what we call the theater of the absurd. This designation is rather general and vague, if you think about it...suggesting that a play is full of characters who are not logical, who attack our sense of rationality and coherence, who mystify us and confuse us. These characters are odd and bizarre, their actions generally strike us as nonsensical and foolish, their behavior is often futile, and they suggest a world devoid of sense and meaning.

On the Origins of the Play

Ionesco describes the curious coincidences that led to the writing of *The Bald Soprano*. He writes (quoted in Richard Coe's book on Ionesco):

> In 1948, before writing my first play, *La Cantatrice chauve*, I had no intentions of becoming a dramatist. My sole ambition was to learn English...and so, with this end in view, I slipped out one day, some eight or ten years ago now, and bought a French-English conversational handbook for beginners [specifically, the *Method Assimil*]. I settled down to work. Conscientiously I set to, and copied out from my handbook lists of "conversational phrases," in order to learn them by heart. But as soon as I came to read them through, I found myself learning, not English, but a series of startling truths: that there are seven days in the week, for instance (which, incidentally, I knew already); or that the floor is *below*, whereas the ceiling is *above*—another phenomenon of which I was basically aware, perhaps, but which I had never seriously reflected upon, or else had simply gone and forgotten, and which now appeared to me, suddenly, as a blinding revelation: astounding, and yet indisputably *true*. (in Coe, 1970, 39)

What Ionesco learned from reading the *Assimil* book of conversational phrases had considerable implications.

They suggested a world full of people who have nothing to say, whose lives are relatively sterile—emotionless and passionless. Ionesco took these phrases and the characters these phrases implied and put them on the stage. When he changed the context, from learning basic phrases needed to get by when traveling, to that of a play frame—the absurdity of the characters' lives and the banality of the topics of their conversation generated laughter and a new genre of theater.

Ionesco used the phrases in the phrase book as an indicator of the mindset and belief structure of the people who would be uttering these phrases, once they learned them. What the *Assimil* book did was suggest what topics are important to ordinary people, what they have to know in order to get by in the modern world—and when Ionesco looked at the world through the prism of his phrase book, he discovered a world of overwhelming banality and nonsense.

Mr. and Mrs. Smith and the Problem of Rationality

The play begins by attacking our sense of rationality. The clock has struck seventeen times and Mrs. Smith says, in the first line of the play, "There, it's nine o'clock." Having the clock strike seventeen times is, in itself, an affront to our understanding of the world, in which clocks never strike more than twelve times. And then, having Mrs. Smith say it is nine o'clock leads to confusion. The audience has heard the clock strike many times and her line about it being nine o'clock doesn't make sense.

So, in the very first line, Ionesco is attacking our understanding of the world and sense of rationality. Next, he addresses the banality and sterility of life in general, and of middle-class life in suburban England in particular.

> MRS. SMITH: We've drunk the soup, and eaten the fish and chips, and the English salad. The children have drunk English water. We've eaten well this evening. That's because we live in the suburbs of London and because our name is Smith.
>
> MR. SMITH: [*continues to read, clicks his tongue.*]

While Mrs. Smith talks, Mr. Smith only continues his reading, and responds to her comments by clicking his tongue. In addition to making generic and bland comments about things, Mrs. Smith also speaks in a style we might describe as primer style, which is made up, for the most part, of short, simple sentences, with few transitions.

> MRS. SMITH: The fish was fresh. It made my mouth water. I had two helpings. No, three helpings. That made me go to the w.c. You also had three help-

The Devices of Absurdity: *The Bald Soprano* 99

ings. However, the third time you took less than the first two times, while as for me, I took a great deal more. I eat better than you this evening. Why is that? Usually, it is you who eats more. It is not appetite you lack.

Primer-style writing makes Mrs. Smith childlike and also reduces readers (and playgoers) to a childish state. Ionesco has used the phrases in the phrase book more or less as they are listed in the book, inserting them into dialogue—where they are appear silly and stupid. Mrs. Smith mentions a Rumanian grocer with a very strange name, Popesco Rosenfeld, who has just come from Constantinople and is a yogurt specialist.

> MRS. SMITH: Yogurt is excellent for the stomach, the kidneys, the appendicitis, and apotheosis.

Ionesco is doing a number of things here. First, he is using the technique of comic cataloging, in which a list of incongruous items is used to create humor. In addition, he has Mrs. Smith make grammatical mistakes and utter malapropisms. She should have said "the appendix" instead of *appendicitis*, to maintain parallelism, and the term "apotheosis" is out of place and nonsensical. This is followed by her mention of Doctor Mackenzie-King, who never prescribes medicine he hasn't tried out on himself. Before operating on a certain Parker's liver, he operated on his own liver, even though he wasn't ill.

On the Uses and Abuses of Logic

When Mr. Smith utters his first lines, asking why Parker died and the doctor pulled through, she replies "Because the operation was successful in the doctor's case and it was not in Parker's." What we have here is a seeming reply but, in fact, merely a different way of saying the same thing—namely that Parker died because his operation was not successful.

> MR. SMITH: A conscientious doctor must die with his patient if they can't get well together. The captain of a ship goes down with his ship into the briny deep, he does not survive alone.

Mrs. Smith says one shouldn't compare a patient to a ship, but Mr. Smith replies that one can, since ships also have diseases like humans, and that doctors should die with their patients just as captains go down with their ships. Mrs. Smith asks what conclusions he draws from his analysis.

MR. SMITH: All doctors are quacks. And all patients too. Only the Royal Navy is honest in England.
MRS. SMITH: But not sailors.
MRS. SMITH: Naturally. [*A pause. Still reading his paper.*] Here's a thing I don't understand. In the newspaper they always give the age of deceased persons but never the age of the newly born. That doesn't make sense.

Ionesco has now started toying, more directly, with our sense of logic, forcing us to consider the nature of rationality. We see, for example, that Ionesco creates a ridiculous analogy—between doctors and captains of ships—which leads to illogical conclusions. Next, he reveals Mr. Smith's ignorance. He can understand why the age of deceased persons is given but not why the age of newborns isn't given. We have a crazy comparison here: involving the disclosure of the ages of dead people but not of newly born people, an idea that is patently ridiculous.

On the Death of Bobby Watson

Mr. Smith then comments on a notice in the paper.

MR. SMITH: [*still reading his paper*]: Tsk, it says here that Bobby Watson died.
MRS. SMITH: My God, the poor man! When did he die?
MR. SMITH: Why do you pretend to be astonished? You know very well that he's been dead these past two years. Surely you remember that we attended his funeral a year and a half ago.

When Mrs. Smith asks him why he was surprised to read it in the paper, he replies that it wasn't in the paper and that it's been three years since his death was announced. He adds that he remembered it through an association of ideas.

Mrs. Smith adds that Bobby Watson was well-preserved.

MR. SMITH: He was the handsomest corpse in Great Britain. He didn't look his age. Poor Bobby, he'd been dead for four years and he was still warm. A veritable living corpse. And how cheerful he was!

There are a number of things occurring here. First, we have the matter of incremental exaggeration, as Mr. Smith keeps adding to the number of years Bobby Watson has been dead. This technique is very similar to that of Falstaff, who describes his heroic battle to Hal and keeps exaggerating the number of people he fought with. Then Ionesco adds a some-

The Devices of Absurdity: *The Bald Soprano*

what macabre contradiction: Bobby Watson is a "veritable living corpse," who was "cheerful." This contradiction confuses us, since we all know that a person is either alive or dead. Ionesco then adds to the confusion, since as it turns out, there are many Bobby Watsons.

The Many Bobby Watsons

When Mrs. Smith replied "Poor Bobby" her husband asks her which Bobby Watson she means.

> MRS. SMITH: It is his wife that I mean. She is called Bobby too, Bobby Watson. Since they both had the same name, you could never tell one from the other when you saw them together. It was only after his death that you could really tell which was which. And there are still people today who confuse her with the deceased and offer their condolences to him. Do you know her?

Mr. Smith replies that he saw her at Bobby Watson's burial.

> MR. SMITH: She has regular features and yet one cannot say that she is pretty. She is too big and stout. Her features are not regular but one can say that she is very pretty. She is a little too small and too thin.

What Ionesco is doing here is using contradictions to confuse the reader. We have a Bobby Watson whose features are regular one moment and not regular the next, who is big and stout one moment and too small and thin the next. It is through these techniques that Ionesco establishes a frame of reference that we describe as absurd—one in which the rules of logic do not apply, where paradoxes are the rule of the day.

The discussion then turns to the impending marriage of Bobby Watson's widow, who, we are told, didn't have children, and then later, did have children (a boy and girl, each named Bobby Watson) and a different Bobby Watson. In addition, the young Bobby Watson has a wealthy uncle, Bobby Watson, who might pay for Bobby Watson's education. The confusion continues in the dialogue that follows.

> MRS. SMITH: That would be proper. And Bobby Watson's aunt, old Bobby Watson, might very well, in her turn, pay for the education of Bobby Watson, Bobby Watson's daughter. That way Bobby, Bobby Watson's mother, could remarry. Has she anyone in mind?
>
> MR. SMITH: Yes, a cousin of Bobby Watson.
>
> MRS. SMITH: Who? Bobby Watson?

Mr. Smith:	Which Bobby Watson do you mean?
Mrs. Smith:	Why, Bobby Watson, the son of old Bobby Watson, the late Bobby Watson's other uncle.
Mr. Smith:	No, it's not that one, it's someone else. It's Bobby Watson, the son of old Bobby Watson, the late Bobby Watson's aunt.
Mrs. Smith:	Are you referring to Bobby Watson the commercial traveler?
Mr. Smith:	All the Bobby Watsons are commercial travelers.

We have so many Bobby Watsons here that nobody can keep track of what is going on—neither the reader nor, it seems, the characters. The particular technique at work here is coincidence. It is a bizarre coincidence that so many characters are named Bobby Watson—Ionesco uses this repetition to intensify the confusion and chaos. When we discuss people, we use their names; since so many people have the same name, it becomes impossible to keep track of who (that is which Bobby Watson) is being talked about.

This passage raises the question of identity and its relationship to our names and occupations. When you have a number of people with the same name and the same occupation, is not personal identity somewhat confused and compromised?

Ionesco turns from this madness about Bobby Watson to a subversion of logic, and more precisely, deductive logic and empiricism, in two celebrated scenes: in one, the Martins discover that they are married to one another and in another, the doorbell rings but when someone opens the door, nobody is there.

Ionesco on the Matter of Deduction

The maid, Mary, announces that the Martins, some friends of the Smiths, have come to visit. The Smiths then leave the stage to change clothes. In his notes, Ionesco states that the dialogue between the Martins should be "drawling, monotonous, a little singsong, without nuances."

Mr. Martin tells Mrs. Martin that he believes he's met her before and she replies that she believes she's met him before. They both discover they are from Manchester.

Mrs. Martin:	That is curious!
Mr. Martin:	Isn't that curious! Only, I, madam, I left the city of Manchester about five weeks ago.

MRS. MARTIN: That is curious! What a bizarre coincidence! I, too, sir, I left the city of Manchester about five weeks ago.

The Martins discover that they took the same train to London, that they both took second class seats, that they both were in coach number 8, compartment 6, had seats opposite one another, and that they both live at 19 Bromfield Street, in apartment 8 on the fifth floor. In addition, they both have a bed with a green eiderdown covering it.

MR. MARTIN: How bizarre, curious, strange! Then, madam, we live in the same room and we sleep in the same bed, dear lady. It is perhaps there that we have met!

She replies that it is possible, but she doesn't recall it. He adds, then, that he has a little daughter named Alice, who is two years old, and has a white eye and a red eye. She says that she also has a two-year-old daughter named Alice with a white eye and a red eye. Mr. Martin replies: "...I believe there can be no doubt about it, we have seen each other before and you are my own wife...Elizabeth, I have found you again!" The Martins embrace.

Mary, the maid, however, tells us that the Martins have made a mistake, and offers proof. Donald Martin's daughter, she says, has a white right eye and a red left eye but Elizabeth's daughter has a red right eye and a white left eye.

MARY ...Thus all of Donald's system of deduction collapses when it comes up against this last obstacle which destroys his whole theory. In spite of the extraordinary coincidences which seem to be definitive proofs, Donald and Elizabeth, not being the parents of the same child, are not Donald and Elizabeth.

She elaborates on this matter and concludes: "My real name is Sherlock Holmes."

Ionesco has parodied the process of logical deduction. The Martins, we must remember, do not recognize one another and thus have to figure out, by a process of deduction, that they are, in fact, married to one another. It is all the "curious" coincidences that the Martins discover that lead them to their great insight. When Mary tells us her real name is Sherlock Holmes, we are reminded, once again, what has been transpiring and that it is the process of deduction that Ionesco has been ridiculing.

The Problem of Empiricism

Having disposed of deduction, Ionesco next turns his attention to empiricism. The Martins are chatting awkwardly with the Smiths in their living room. The conversation is banal and moronic, punctuated by awkward silences. Ionesco brings up the subject of logic once again.

MRS. SMITH: The heart is ageless. [*Silence.*]
MR. MARTIN: That's true. [*Silence.*]
MRS. SMITH: So they say. [*Silence.*]
MRS. MARTIN: They also say the opposite. [*Silence.*]
MR. SMITH: The truth lies somewhere between the two. [*Silence.*]

Mr. Smith's reply—that the truth lies somewhere between two contradictory statements—is the kind of statement people often make when dealing with contradictions, although it is incorrect. The couples then get into a discussion that eventuates in one person interrupting another. They are squabbling about that when the doorbell rings. Mrs. Smith goes to see who is at the door but doesn't find anyone. Then the doorbell rings again. Mrs. Smith goes to the door for the second time and doesn't find anyone there, so she sits down. The doorbell rings for the third time.

MRS. SMITH: I'm not going to open the door again.
MR. SMITH: Yes, but there must be someone there!
MRS. SMITH: The first time there was no one. The second time, no one. Why do you think there is someone there now?
MR. SMITH: Because someone has rung!
MRS. MARTIN: That's no reason.
MR. MARTIN: What? When one hears the doorbell ring that means someone is at the door ringing to have the door opened.
MRS. MARTIN: Not always. You've just seen otherwise!
MR. MARTIN: In most cases, yes.
MR. SMITH: As for me, when I go to visit someone, I ring in order to be admitted. I think that everyone does the same thing and that each time there is a ring there must be someone there.
MRS. SMITH: That is true in theory. But in reality things happen differently. You have just seen otherwise.

Here Ionesco ridicules scientific method and empiricism, which are based on the careful observation of experience. Deductive logic, as reflected in Mrs. Smith's comments, tells us that when a doorbell rings, someone is ringing the doorbell to get admitted. But Mrs. Smith counters that experience proves otherwise. She went to the door three times after the doorbell has rung and has not found anyone there. Therefore she concludes that when the doorbell rings, nobody is there.

The doorbell rings again for the fourth time. Mrs. Smith refuses to answer it.

> MRS. SMITH: [*in a fit of anger*]: Don't send me to open the door again. You've seen that it was useless. Experience teaches us that when one hears the doorbell ring it is because there is never anyone there.

There is a dispute between the women and the men about whether anyone is there when the doorbell rings. Mrs. Smith finally goes to the door and finds the Fire Chief. This confuses matters greatly, since Mrs. Smith has argued that when the doorbell rings there is never anybody there, whereas Mr. Smith has argued that each time the doorbell rings there is always somebody there. She adds that her position has been proved "not by theoretical demonstrations but by facts." When Mr. Smith counters that the fire chief is there, she says that this doesn't disprove her case, because he was there only when the bell rang for the fourth time and "the fourth time does not count."

This leads to the interrogation of the fire chief, who says that he was standing at the door for three quarters of an hour. He adds, when questioned, that he did not ring the bell the first two times, but did the third time, after which he hid himself as a joke. He offers a solution to the question of whether anyone is at the door when it rings.

> FIRE CHIEF: I am going to reconcile you. You both are partly right. When the doorbell rings, sometimes there is someone, other times there is no one.
> MR. MARTIN: This seems logical to me.
> MRS. MARTIN: I think so too.

The fire chief asks whether they would like to hear any of his stories. The Smiths and Martins say yes. Mrs. Smith says that his stories are "all true, and they are based on experience." He adds that he speaks from his own experience and offers "truth, nothing but the truth." What follows are some incomprehensible stories, such as "The Dog and the Cow" and "The Cock." His last story, "The Headcold," uses a discursive style, that keeps going off on tangents, to generate its humor.

FIRE CHIEF: "The Headcold." My brother-in law had, on the paternal side, a first cousin whose maternal uncle had a father-in-law whose paternal grandfather had married as his second wife....

After this story, the play turns toward the overt use of nonsense, wordplay, playing with sounds and that kind of thing. For example, Mary recites a poem, in honor of the fire chief, that uses repetition, nonsense and banality to create humor.

MARY: "The Fire"
The polypoids were burning in the wood
A stone caught fire
The castle caught fire
The forest caught fire...

and so on, with even the fire catching fire.

The fire chief tells everyone he has to leave, since there will be a fire occurring at the other end of the city in "exactly three-quarters of an hour and sixteen minutes."

MRS. MARTIN: Thanks to you we have passed a truly Cartesian quarter of an hour.
FIRE CHIEF: [*moving towards the door, then stopping*]: Speaking of that—the bald soprano? [*General silence, embarrassment.*]
MRS. SMITH: She always wears her hair in the same style.

After the fire chief has left, the Martins and the Smiths have a dialogue with one another in terms of mock folk sayings, proverbs that don't make any sense.

MR. MARTIN: He who sells an ox today, will have an egg tomorrow.
MRS. SMITH: In real life, one must look out the window.
MRS. MARTIN: One can sit down on a chair, when the chair doesn't have any.

Ionesco inserts stage directions to the effect that both couples recite their lines in a hostile manner and by the end of the scene are screaming at one another hysterically, with fists raised.

MR. SMITH: Cockatoos, cockatoos, cockatoos, cockatoos, cockatoos, cockatoos, cockatoos, cockatoos, cockatoos, cockatoos.
MRS. SMITH: Such caca, such caca, such caca, such caca, such caca, such caca, such caca, such caca.
MRS. MARTIN: Such cascades of cacas, such cascades of cacas, such cascades of cacas, such cascades of cacas, such cascades of cacas, such cascades of cacas, such cascades of cacas.

The Devices of Absurdity: *The Bald Soprano* 107

This type of dialogue is followed by playing with words and sounds and is quite regressive, reminding one of the way children play with sounds and words.

MRS. MARTIN: Don't ruche my brooch!
MR. MARTIN: Don't smooch the brooch!
MR. SMITH: Groom the goose, don't goose the groom.

and later:

MR. SMITH: Seducer seduced!
MRS. MARTIN: Scaramouche!
MRS. SMITH: Sainte-Nitouche!
MR. MARTIN: Go take a douche.

They move to playing with the names of poets, reciting vowels and consonants. Mrs. Smith imitates a train, "choo, choo, choo…" and they finally end up yelling "it's not that way, it's over here" again and again as the lights dim and after they have gone out.

When the lights come on we find that the Martins are now seated like the Smiths were in the beginning of the play and that the Martins are now saying the same lines as the Smiths; the play is continuing, returning to the beginning, in an infinite regress with different characters, as the curtain falls, ending the play.

On the Matter of Absurdity

Ionesco has used, with considerable brilliance and imagination, a large number of comic techniques to create his "absurd theater." We find a number of linguistic techniques such as infantilism, puns and wordplay, definition and misunderstanding. But it is with logical techniques that Ionesco has been preoccupied. He uses contradiction frequently, when one character makes a statement and later contradicts the statement or another character contradicts the original statement. Thus Mr. Smith describes Bobby Watson's widow as both too big and stout and too small and too thin.

He also utilizes nonsense, especially at the end of the play, when the characters talk gibberish. For example, after playing with "ouche" sounds (as in douche, Sainte-Nitouche, Scaramouche) Mr. Smith starts with "ope" sounds and says "The pope elopes. The pope's got no horoscope. The horoscope's bespoke."

We also find the technique of ignorance, when characters make malapropisms or don't recognize their own husbands or wives and have to use the process of deduction to discover that they are married to one another. Ionesco uses repetition with great skill. Many of the lines are repetitious, as in the "Fire" poem, and even the play, itself starts repeating as the curtain falls.

A great deal of the play involves ridiculing the way people in England are so obsessed by things English (found in the description of the play's opening scene) and the banality of everyday life in the English (and by extension all middle-class) suburbs. He parodies, mercilessly, the foundations on which we all structure our sense of how the world works—deductive reasoning and empiricism. He creates characters who are so banal, their lives reflecting the concerns of people shown in language books, that they are ultimately eccentric grotesques. They cannot communicate with one another effectively, and are, Ionesco suggests, ultimately, ciphers that can be replaced by anyone else—that is, by other ciphers.

I consider absurdity to be a technique used to create humor, a technique based on subverting logic, uttering contradictory statements, offering paradoxes that we cannot fathom, speaking nonsense and that kind of thing. Ionesco, and others like him, take the technique of absurdity to new heights and use various strategies that confuse the reader of the play, generate a state of bemusement, disorientation, and wonderment.

Ionesco recognized the comic potentialities in language books for tourists; that is, he was able to see the absurd nature of the topics dealt with in these books and the limited and sterile nature of the life they suggest: you can take the books literally, on one hand (and learn that ceilings are up and floors are down), but you can also use the books as signifiers of a certain perspective on life on the other hand.

Ionesco exaggerates the banality of the traveler's everyday concerns, and, at the same time, decontextualizes the worldview presented in language books. This, when coupled with his masterful use of the techniques of humor, yielded a play that is both hilarious and bewildering, that makes us laugh while, at the same time, it subverts our sense of rationality.

The Bald Soprano is not a conventional comedy, like *Miles Gloriosus* or *The School for Scandal* in that it does not have a plot involving lovers who are separated and have to get together (though the Martins might be classified as such, since both have amnesia and have to use deductive

The Devices of Absurdity: *The Bald Soprano*

reason to find that they are married to one another), or in which there is a complication in the plot that has to be resolved by trickery or cleverness.

Instead, the play contains a series of vignettes, so to speak, in which Ionesco parodies deductive and inductive logic and ridicules any number of other things. It does, like most comedies, have eccentric or perhaps "ridiculous" (to satisfy Aristotle) characters who, one way or another, survive, unlike tragic characters who are usually carried off, dead, at the end of the play. One might argue that the characters actually are, in their banality and emptiness, tragic figures of sorts, but I would suggest, going back to Aristotle, that ridiculous figures are comic ones, even if there may be tragic aspects to their lives.

Ionesco puts a darker perspective on things. He describes the play as follows:

> The text of *La Cantatrice chauve*, or rather of my handbook of English...being made up, as it was, of ready-made expressions, of the most threadbare platitudes imaginable, revealed to me, by this very fact, the secret of "talking and saying nothing," the secret of talking and saying nothing *because there is nothing personal to say*, the absence of any inner life, the mechanical soullessness of daily routine: man totally absorbed in his social context, and indistinguishable from it. The Smiths and Martins have forgotten how to talk because they have forgotten how to think; and they have forgotten how to think *because they have forgotten the meaning of emotion, because they are devoid of passions*. (in Coe, 1970, 40–41)

Ultimately, the characters in the play are part of a world so impersonal that the characters in it are interchangeable, which is the way that Ionesco ends the play.

Ionesco's self-described "anti-play" was first produced in 1950. Unfortunately, it seems that the world, and the various lead and supporting players in it, are just as absurd as his Smiths and Martins. Indeed, by seeing the difficulties the Smiths and Martin have in communicating with one another and making sense of the world, in seeing the utter banality of their lives, we can perhaps better understand why things are the way they are. We change the characters, from time to time, but the madness, Ionesco tells us, goes on and on.

6

Beyond Devices

In this book I have argued that all humor stems from the use of forty-five techniques that, in various combinations, generate smiles, mirth, laughter—whatever you wish to call it—which signify that someone or some group of people found something humorous. (To simplify things, I will take laughter as a signifier of humor, even though I realize this is somewhat reductionistic.)

In addition, I have shown how the great comedy playwrights have all used these forty-five techniques of humor, but it is *how* these techniques are used that separates writers of genius from mediocrities. We all use the same words (more or less) as Shakespeare, but we don't use them as well as he did—or the other playwrights I have dealt with in this book, such as Ben Jonson, Tom Stoppard, and Eugene Ionesco.

I am not suggesting that any of these playwrights articulated a typology of humor as extensive as mine or were conscious of all of these techniques. Nor do I suggest that comedians and humorists are aware of all the techniques that are available to them. (But comedy writers must be aware that in certain situations, various "techniques" of humor work and generate laughter.) Rather, I suggest that a content analysis of humorous texts—of all sorts—shows that there are only a relatively limited number of techniques that playwrights (and other kinds of humorists) use to create humor and laughter. There may only be forty-five techniques but since they all are used, generally speaking, in various combinations, the number of possibilities is enormous.

On the Social Significance of Techniques

Many of these techniques that I have been discussing have, as it turns out, social and political implications. Consider, for example, such techniques as allusions, exaggerations, stereotypes, insults, parodies, and satires. These techniques often rely upon social and political events to work. A braggart soldier like Miles Gloriosus suggests to us, by implication, that many soldiers brag and that we must take our soldiers' stories with a grain of salt. In addition, laughing at a foolish soldier ultimately leads to a lack of respect for authority figures of all kinds and that attitude has political significance.

Stereotypes deal with groups and subcultures in society and tend to reflect the attitudes of dominant groups towards various ethnic, racial, sexual, and other minorities. These stereotypes tend to be negative and highly insulting at times, though they are often camouflaged by humor.

Thus in Trevor Griffiths's *Comedians* we find Waters, who is instructing some students who want to become comedians, on the use of stereotypes. He offers, in rapid succession, stereotypes of the Irish ("Big, thick, stupid head, large cabbage ears, hairy nostrils, daft eyes, fat flapping hands..."); of Jews ("Grafters. Fixers. Money. Always money. Say Jew, say gold. Moneylenders, pawn-brokers, usurers...."); and of workers ("Dirty. Unschooled. Shifty. Grabbing all they can get. Putting coal in the bath. Chips with everything.... Breeding like rabbits, sex-mad. And their mean, vicious womenfolk, driving them on. Animals, to be fed slops and fastened up at night...."). We can see that stereotypes often make use of insults and, if taken out of the play-frame context, are not funny at all. But even in the play-frame situation, when we realize that the insulting stereotypes are not to be taken "seriously," the aggression in stereotypes often is so strong that listeners are offended.

When you get to satire, which I have listed as a technique (that employs other techniques, such as insult, ridicule, imitation, etc.) there is obviously a social dimension to the humor. Satire breeds on political folly and social stupidity and has often been interpreted as being an indirect way to criticize and suggest alternatives to the social and political order that is satirized.

Comedy is social and the dramatic comedies we have examined in this book tell us a great deal about the societies in which they were written. We learn interesting things about important individuals, about the political order, about social tensions and a variety of other matters. That is why laughter by audiences can be seen as, in many cases, a kind of rough equivalent of an opinion poll.

Laughter is social. We know that laughter is also contagious—which is why situation comedies use canned laughter—to help audiences laugh at "appropriate" times and convince audiences that what they have seen is funny. The use of laugh-tracks started in 1950, when a comedy program used a laugh track to take the place of a live audience.

A Disquisition on Laughter

We all (with rare exceptions) laugh a number of times during a typical day. Curiously enough, until fairly recently, the matter of what laughter is was not investigated to any great degree of thoroughness. This lack has been rectified by the work of a psychologist, Robert Provine, who published an excellent article in *American Scientist* entitled "Laughter."

In this article Provine explains that laughter is a "social vocalization of the human animal" and defines it as follows:

> A laugh is characterized by a series of short vowel-like notes syllables), each about 75 milliseconds long, that are repeated at regular intervals about 210 milliseconds apart. A specific vowel sound does not define laughter, but similar vowel sounds are typically used for the notes of a given laugh. For example, laughs have the structure "ha-ha-ha-ha" or "ho-ho-ho-ho" but not "ha-ho-ha-ho." (1996, 39)

One important thing that Provine discovered in his study of laughter is that most laughter comes from banal remarks rather than structured jokes. As he explains (1996, 41), "Mutual playfulness, in-group feeling and positive emotional tone—not comedy—mark the social settings of most naturally occurring laughter."

He adds that laughter tends to be randomly scattered throughout our speech and that there is reason to believe that laughter is also connected to matters such as dominance and submission, acceptance and rejection.

Laughter, then, is physiological, in the sense that an individual laughs and that this laughter has a particular structure to it in all humans. But it is also social and political. It takes place, generally speaking, in group situations and is contagious—that is, it is affected by the laughter of others. If laughter (and humor) is involved with dominance and submission, as Provine suggests, there is obviously a political and social dimension to it. We can use humor to attack those in authority and those in authority can use humor to coerce those under them. It can be used as a means of social control, but it also can be used as a means of resistance to this control.

The fact that most laughter does not come from jokes lends support to my contention that the best way to create humor is by using the techniques of humor randomly, in conversations, rather than by telling jokes—which I define as narratives, meant to amuse, with punch lines. When you tell a joke you are usually performing someone else's material. When you use techniques like exaggeration, repartee, insult, and imitation, you are creating (so to speak) your own material, and this material is usually something that pops into your head and which is tied to some ongoing conversation. I am not arguing that jokes are not funny—some of them are, and when told by a good joke teller, they are a source of great delight. Unfortunately many jokes are not particularly funny, in some cases people have already heard the joke, and most people do not tell jokes well. People who are perceived as "funny" by others generally, I would suggest, are people who have learned to use a few techniques of humor well: wit, absurdity, exaggeration, comparisons, and so on.

On Comedy and Tragedy

Let me say something about the difference between comedy and tragedy (drawing on material found in my book *An Anatomy of Humor*). It is a commonplace that tragedy is personal and comedy is social. This means that tragedies generally deal with some great and powerful individual who is destroyed, while comedies deal with common and lowly types who get themselves into messes but survive.

The world of comedy is the world of freedom—of chance and coincidence, while the world of tragedy is one of determinism—as the tragic figures move towards their inevitable destruction. Comic figures tend to be low ones—fools, churls, country bumpkins, gluttons, and so on—while tragic figures are generally elevated ones—persons of consequence. Comedy, then, is optimistic. Comic figures get into messes and, one way or another, often after various humiliations, find ways to survive them. Tragic figures move, ineluctably, towards their destruction, so it can be argued that tragedy is pessimistic. Most tragedies end with the tragic figures dead.

For some reason, perhaps because of the catharsis audiences experience when they watch tragedies, tragedies have traditionally been seen as more elevated, more important kinds of works than comedies. Comedies provide pleasure, which is always suspect, and tragedies provide pain, as we watch characters destroy themselves or be destroyed by others. ("Pain" is too simple a term, for we also experience many other things when we watch a great tragedy. But since I'm dealing with polar oppositions, I have used the term.)

Let me show these relationships in the following chart:

THE COMIC	**THE TRAGIC**
The Social	The Individual
Freedom	Determinism
Chance	Inevitability
Survival	Destruction
Lowly Characters	Elevated Characters
Low Status	High Status
Optimistic	Pessimistic
Knowledge	Insight
Pleasure	Pain
Cathexis	Catharsis

The comic heroes and heroines provide cathexis, which I understand to mean the liberation of pent-up energy, which often has a sexual dimension to it. Many comedies involve the triumph of young lovers who have to overcome various obstacles provided by old men (senex figures) and social conventions.

M.M. Bakhtin, the eminent Russian scholar, has argued that laughter destroys hierarchical distancing and thus implicitly has an egalitarian edge to it. As he explains in *The Dialogical Imagination*:

> Laughter demolishes fear and piety before an object, before a world, making of it an object of familiar contact and thus clearing the ground for an absolutely free investigation of it. Laughter is a vital factor in laying down the prerequisite for fearlessness without which it would be impossible to approach the world realistically. (1981, 231)

So laughter, Bakhtin argues, plays an important role in helping us look at the world realistically and is a kind of catalytic agent that generates creativity and knowledge.

Thus, in addition to its social and political dimensions, humor helps us understand ourselves and the world we live in. In this comedies differ from tragedies, which offer us insights of great depth into ourselves and into what might be described as the human condition. Comic laughter can be seen, then, not as an escape from society and the outside world but as an encounter with it and, to the extent that comic characters survive and that comedies end on a happy note (often with a marriage), a triumph over it.

On Comedy Writing and Code Violations

Comedy writing is the most difficult kind of writing there is. The plots of comedies are much more complicated, as a rule, than those of tragedies. In comedies, characters get into messes and have to extricate themselves from them; in tragedies, the plots are relatively simple—characters either self-destruct or are destroyed by others (or there is a combination of the two). It is much easier to make people cry than it is to make them laugh.

Comedies tend to be about types of characters: buffoons, churls, lovesick suitors, haughty women, shrews, misers, fools, and so on. The term "types" suggests the social dimension of comedy. Each character in a comedy is an individual, but these individuals fall into various categories; thus, when we watch a fool, we measure that fool against the image we have, in our mind's eye, of what fools should be like—what we might call Platonic, idealized fools. The same applies to all of the comic types. We see individual characters as "figures" against the "ground" of comedic conventions and comic types that we have all learned.

These comic figures violate certain codes we believe to be normal and reasonable in individuals. So comedies involve, to a great degree, figures who violate social and cultural codes. Let me suggest some of these in the chart below.

COMIC ASPECT	CODE VIOLATED
Type	Individuality
Liars, Frauds	Truthfulness
Eccentrics	Normalcy
Monomaniacs	Flexibility
Crazies	Rationality
Obsessives	Reasonableness
Braggarts, Megalomaniacs	Modesty
Swindlers	Justice

Our comic types are people who are out of step with social norms and must, at the end of their adventures, either be brought back into the fold, after having suffered various humiliations, or be recognized for what they are and held up to public ridicule.

And just as the writers of comedies often use a number of different techniques when they write, so do their comic characters often exhibit a number of code violations. Thus, obsessional types such as misers are also, as we see with Volpone, liars and frauds. And both Volpone, and his servant Mosca—both swindlers—are ultimately discovered and punished.

Conclusions

In this book I have suggested that there is a limited number of techniques that comedy writers can use to generate humor. No playwrights use all of them, but many playwrights use a goodly number of them. Moreover, these techniques have been used for thousands of years. I have shown that Plautus, William Shakespeare, Ben Jonson, and Eugene Ionesco used them and also quoted from a number of other contemporary and not-so-contemporary playwrights who have used them in their works.

What is important, of course, is how these techniques are used. The great playwrights use them brilliantly, as the examples in the book demonstrate. I hope that this book will be of use to those who wish to create humor, by suggesting how they can use the forty-five techniques of humor I elicited from my content analysis of works of humor. I hope, also, this book will be of use to those who wish to study humor, by showing how some of the greatest playwrights have used these techniques. In my mind, creativity and analysis work hand in hand, and this book, with its examples and its analyses, provides the opportunity for those who read it to be more analytic and thus, ultimately, more creative.

A General Bibliography of Humor

Note: Plays by William Shakespeare, Ben Johnson, Oscar Wilde, and the other playwrights cited whose works are in the public domain are widely available, so I have not specified any particular edition.

Adams, J. *Ethnic Humor*. New York: Manor Books, 1975.
Allen, S. *Funny Man*. New York: Simon & Schuster, 1956.
Apte, M.L. *Humor and Laughter: An Anthropological Approach*. Ithaca, NY: Cornell University Press, 1985.
Alter, Robert. *Rogue's Progress*. Cambridge, MA: Harvard University Press, 1964.
Ashbee, C.R. *Caricature*. London: Chapman & Hall, Ltd., 1928.
Ausubel, Nathan. *A Treasury of Jewish Humor*. New York: Doubleday, 1951.
Bakhtin, Mikhail. *The Dialogic Imagination*. Edited by Michael Holquist and translated by Caryl Emerson and Michael Holquist. Austin, TX: University of Texas Press, 1981.
Bakhtin, Mikhail. *Rabelais and His World*. Translated by Helene Iswolsky. Bloomington, IN: Indiana University Press, 1984.
Becker, Stephen. *Comic Art in America*. New York: Simon & Schuster, 1959.
Beckett, Samuel. *Krapp's Last Tape and Other Dramatic Pieces*. New York: Grove Press, 1960.
Berger, Arthur Asa. *Li'l Abner: A Study in American Satire*. New York: Twayne Publishers, 1970.
———. *The Comic-Stripped American*. New York: Walker & Co., 1973.
———, ed. "Humor, The Psyche, and Society." *American Behavioral Scientist*, 30, no. 3 (January/February 1987).
———. *An Anatomy of Humor*. New Brunswick, NJ: Transaction Publishers, 1993.
———. *Blind Men and Elephants: Perspectives on Humor*. New Brunswick, NJ: Transaction Publishers, 1995.
Bergler, Edmund. *Laughter and the Sense of Humor*. New York: Intercontinental Medical Book Co., 1956.
Blair, Walter. *Native American Humor*. San Francisco, CA: Chandler Publishing Co., 1960.

Boatright, Moady. *Folk Laughter on the American Frontier.* New York: Collier Books, 1961.

Boskin, J. *Humor and Social Change in Twentieth Century America.* Boston: The Public Library of the City of Boston, 1979.

Botkin, B.A. *A Treasury of American Folklore.* New York: Crown Publishers, 1944.

Chapman, Tony and Hugh Foot, eds. *Humor and Laughter: Theory, Research and Applications* London: John Wiley & Sons, 1976.

Charney, Maurice. *Comedy High & Low.* New York: Oxford Univ. Press, 1978.

Coe, Richard. *Eugene Ionesco: A Study of His Work.* New York: Grove Press, 1970.

Cousins, Norman. *Anatomy of an Illness.* New York: W.W. Norton & Co., 1979.

Davis, Murray S. *What's So Funny: The Comic Conception of Culture and Society.* Chicago: University of Chicago Press, 1993.

Douglas, Mary. *Implicit Meanings: Essays in Anthropology.* London: Routledge & Kegan Paul, 1975.

Duncan, H.D. *Language and Literature in Society.* Chicago: University of Chicago Press, 1953.

Dundes, Alan. *Cracking Jokes: Studies of Sick Humor Cycles and Stereotypes.* Berkeley, CA: Ten Speed Press, 1987.

Ehrenberg, Victor. *The People of Aristophanes: A Sociology of Old Attic Comedy.* New York: Schocken Books, 1962.

Esar, Evan. *The Comic Encyclopedia.* Garden City, NY: Doubleday, 1978.

Felheim, Marvin. Ed. *Comedy: Plays, Theory and Criticism.* New York: Harcourt, Brace & World, Inc., 1962.

Feinberg, Leonard. *The Satirist: His Temperament, Motivation and Influence.* Ames, IA: Iowa State University Press, 1963.

Freud, Sigmund. *Jokes and Their Relation to the Unconscious.* New York: W.W. Norton & Co., 1960.

Fry, William. *Sweet Madness: A Study of Humor.* Palo Alto, CA: Pacific Books, 1963.

Fry, William and Melanie Allen. *Make 'Em Laugh: A Study of Comedy Writers.* Palo Alto, CA: Science & Behavior Books, 1975.

Fry, William and Waleed A. Salameh, eds. *Handbook of Humor and Psychotherapy.* Sarasota, FL: Professional Resource Exchange, 1986.

Frye, Northrop. *Anatomy of Criticism.* Princeton, NJ: Princeton University Press, 1957.

Garber, Marjorie. *Vested Interests: Cross-Dressing and Cultural Anxiety.* New York: HarperPerennial, 1993.

Griffiths, Trevor. *Comedians.* New York: Grove Press, 1976.

Grotjahn, Martin. *Beyond Laughter: Humor and the Subconscious.* New York: McGraw Hill, 1957.
Gruner, Charles. *Understanding Laughter: The Works of Wit and Humor.* Chicago: Nelson-Hall, 1978.
Harrison, Randall. *The Cartoon: Communication to the Quick.* Beverley Hills, CA: SAGE Publications, 1981.
Helitzer, Melvin. *Comedy Writing Secrets.* Cincinnati, OH: Writer's Digest Books, 1987.
Highet, Gilbert. *The Anatomy of Satire.* Princeton, NJ: Princeton University Press, 1962.
Hoffman, Werner. *Caricature from Leonardo to Picasso.* London: John Calder, 1957.
Ionesco, Eugene. *Four Plays.* Translated by Donald M. Allen. New York: Grove Press, 1958.
Jensen, Ejner J. *Shakespeare and the Ends of Comedy.* Bloomington, IN: Indiana University Press, 1991.
Kayser, Wolfgang. *The Grotesque in Art and Literature.* Bloomington, IN: Indiana University Press, 1963.
Klapp, Orrin E. *Heroes, Villains and Fools: The Changing American Character.* Englewood Cliffs, NJ: Prentice-Hall, 1962.
Klein, Allen. *The Healing Power of Humor.* Los Angeles: Jeremy P. Tarcher, 1989.
Kris, Ernst. *Psychoanalytic Explorations in Art.* New York: International University Press, 1952.
Legman, Gershon. *Rationale of the Dirty Joke.* New York: Grove Press, 1968.
Levin, Harry. *Playboys and Killjoys: An Essay on the Theory & Practices of Comedy.* New York: Oxford University Press, 1987.
Levine, Jacob. ed. *Motivation in Humor.* New York: Atherton Press, 1969.
Lynn, Kenneth. *Mark Twain and Southwestern Humor.* Boston, MA: Atlantic Little-Brown, 1959.
McGhee, Paul E. *Humor: Origins and Development.* San Francisco, CA: W.H. Freeman & Co., 1979.
McGhee, Paul E. and Jeffrey H. Goldstein. *The Handbook of Humor Research.* Vol. 1 and 2. New York: Springer-Verlag, 1983.
Mendel, Werner, ed. *A Celebration of Laughter.* Los Angeles: Mara Books, 1970.
Mindess, Harvey. *Laughter and Liberation.* Los Angeles: Nash Publishing, 1971.
Monroe, D.H. *Argument of Laughter.* Melbourne: Melbourne University Press, 1951.
Morreall, J. *Taking Laughter Seriously.* Albany, NY: State University of New York Press, 1983.

Piddington, Ralph. *The Psychology of Laughter.* New York: Gamut Press, 1963.
Plessner, Helmuth. *Laughter and Crying.* Evanston, IL: Northwestern University Press, 1970.
Powell, Chris and George E.C. Paton, eds. *Humour in Society: Resistance and Control.* New York: St. Martin's Press, 1988.
Provine, Robert R. "Laughter." *The American Scientist* 84 (January\February 1996).
Raskin, V. *Semantic Mechanisms of Humor.* Dordecht: D. Reidel, 1985.
Rosenheim, E.W. *Swift and the Satirist's Art.* Chicago: University of Chicago Press, 1963.
Rourke, Constance. *American Humor: A Study of National Character.* New York: Doubleday Anchor Books, 1931.
Simon, Neil. *The Comedy of Neil Simon.* New York: Avon, 1971.
Stoppard, Tom. *Travesties.* New York: Grove Press, 1975.
Sypher, Wylie, ed. *Comedy.* New York: Doubleday Anchor Books, 1956.
Wilson, Christopher P. *Jokes: Form, Content, Use and Function.* London: Academic Press, 1979.
Wolfenstein, Martha. *Children's Humor: A Psychological Analysis.* Bloomington, IN: Indiana University Press, 1954.
Yates, Norris. *The American Humorist: Conscience of the Twentieth Century.* Ames, IA: Iowa State University Press, 1964.
Vernon, Enid, ed. *Humor in America: An Anthology.* New York: Harcourt Brace Jovanovich, 1976.
Ziv, Avner. *Personality and Sense of Humor.* New York: Springer, 1984.

Name Index

Allen, Woody, 23
Aristophanes, 7
Aristotle, 58

Bakhtin, M.M., 115
Barber, C.L., 82
Beckett, Samuel, 16, 17
Benny, Jack, 35
Bergman, Ingmar, 33
Bergson, Henri, 28, 38
Browne, Sir Thomas, 10

Chaplin, Charlie, 42
Coe, Richard, 97, 109

Frye, Northrop, 82

Garber, Marjorie, 75, 76
Griffiths, Trevor, viii, 43, 447 112

Hardy, Oliver, 42
Hemingway, Ernest 1, 33

Ionesco, Eugene, viii, 3, 25, 49, 97–104, 106–109, 111, 117

Jensen, Ejner J., 82
Jonson, Ben, viii, 60, 111, 117
Joyce, James, 6, 7, 26, 27, 30, 33, 34, 41

Keaton, Buster, 12

Laurel, Stan, 42
Lenin, V.I., 7, 30
Levin, Harry, 84

MacDonald Ramsay, 31

Nixon, Richard, 29

Plautus, Titus Maccius, viii, 3, 48, 49, 51, 52, 58, 65, 117
Provine, Robert, 113

Queneau, Raymond, 1, 2

Rabelais, Francois, 69

Shakespeare, William, vii, viii, 3, 6, 15, 17, 30, 34, 39, 49, 65, 75, 81, 827 111, 117
Sheridan, Richard Brinsley, 3, 9, 12, 14, 37, 45, 49, 83, 93, 94
Simon, Neil, vii, viii
Stewart, Jimmy, 29
Stoppard, Tom, viii, 6, 7, 25, 26, 27, 31, 33, 34, 35, 36, 41, 111

Tzara, Tristan, 6, 7, 26, 33, 34, 35

Wayne, John, 29
Wilde, Oscar, viii, 37, 38, 40, 41

Subject Index

Absurdity, 3, 5, 59
    difference from infantilism, 6
Accidents, 3, 5, 34
Agroikos, 48
Alazons, 48, 51, 54
    Greek for for Gloriosus, 54
    Latin for braggart, 54
Allusion, 3, 5
    figure-ground and, 7
Analogies, 3, 5, 8, 13, 58
An Anatomy of Humor, 2
    Bald Soprano, 3, 5, 6, 25, 26, 49, 97–109
    attack on rationality in, 98–100
    comedic coincidence in, 101, 102
    ignorance and stupidity, 108
    infantilism, 107
    lack of emotion in characters, 109
    parody of deduction and logic, 102, 103
    ridiculing the English, 108
    wordplay, 107

Before and After, 3, 5, 8
Birds, 33
Boaster (see Alazon), 48, 51
Body Language, 47
Bombast, 3, 5, 9, 10
Burlesque, 3, 5, 10
    lampoon, 10
    satire, 10
    travesty, 10

Caricature, 3, 5, 10, 11
Catalogues, 3, 5, 11
Chase Scenes, 3, 5, 12
Code Violations
    comedy and, 116
Coincidences, 3, 5, 12, 58

Comedians, 43, 44, 45
Comedic style, 1
Comedy
    code violations and, 116
    difference from tragedy, 114, 115
    discrepant awareness and, 76
    eccentric types, 82
    onomastics and, 84
    social aspects of, 112
Comic Devices in The School for Scandal
    embarrassment, 97
    exposure, 94
    ignorance, 93
    impersonation, 93, 94, 95
Comic types
    dandies, 49
    fops, 49
    gluttons, 49
    misanthropes, 49
    misers, 49
    sex starved men and women, 49
Comparisons, 3, 5, 12, 13, 59
Cops, 12
Creative process
    humor and, viii
Cross-Examination Style, 2

Dada, 7
Defeated Expectations, 15, 16
Definitions, 3, 5, 14, 15
Der Dove, 33
Development, 8
Dialogical Imagination, 115
Disappointments, 3, 5, 15, 16
Discrepant Awareness, 21–23, 72
    comedy and, 76
Double Entry Style, 1
Dramatic Irony, 27

Eccentricity, 3, 5, 16, 58
Eirons, 27, 48, 51, 96
Embarrassment, 3, 5, 17, 18, 59
    escape from, 17, 18, 20
Empiricism and Comedy, 104, 105
Escape from Embarrassment, 17, 18, 20
Exaggeration, 3, 4, 5, 18, 19
Exercises in Style, 1
Exposure, 3, 5, 19, 20

Facetiousness, 3, 5, 20, 21
Facial Expression, 47
Flattery, 63
Fools, 21, 49

Grotesque, 3, 5, 21
Gulls, 48

Henry IV, Part I, 15, 18, 19, 30
Hicks (see Agroikos), 48
Humor
    forty-five techniques of, 1–50
    creative process and, viii
Humor Categories
    action, visual phenomena, 3
    identity, 3
    language, 3
    logic, 3
Humorous Techniques
    social and political implications of, 111–113

Ignorance, Gullability, Naivete, 3, 5, 21–23
Illusion and Reality in Miles Gloriosus, 63
Imitation, 3, 5, 11, 23
Impersonation, 3, 5, 11, 21, 24, 25, 58
Importance of Being Earnest, 37, 38, 40, 41, 42
Infantilism, 3, 5, 25, 26
Insults, 3, 4, 5, 26, 27, 31, 59
    play frame and, 26
Irony, 3, 5, 27, 28, 59
    dramatic, 27
    verbal, 27

Krapp's Last Tape, 16, 17
Krazy Kat, 35

Laughter, 112–114
    definition of, 113
    relation to fearlessness, 115
Literalness, 3, 5, 28, 29

Makeup and Props, 47
Merry Wives of Windsor, 15, 16, 17, 18
Metaphors, 8, 13
Miles Gloriosus, 3, 48, 49, 51–64, 65, 81, 108
    techniques of humor used in, 58, 59
Mimicry, 3, 5, 29, 30
Mistakes, 3, 5, 30, 31, 58, 86
Misunderstanding, 3, 5, 31–33, 63
Monomaniacs as comic, 21, 49
Much Ado About Nothing, 29

Neue Zuricher Zeitung, 36
Noises and Sound Effects, 48
Nonsense, 106

Official Letter Style, 2
Onomastics, 84
    comedy and 84
Over-Literalness, 28

Parody, 1, 3, 4, 5
    genre, 33
    specific text, 33
    style, 33
Pedants, 48, 49
Playboys & Killjoys, 84
Play Frame, 4
Practical jokes, 80, 81
Pretenders (see Eirons), 48 Pretense, 23
Puns, Wordplays, 3, 5, 34, 35

Repartee, 3, 5, 35
Repetition, Pattern, 3, 5, 35, 36
Revelation of Ignorance, 58
Reversal, 3, 5, 36, 37
    difference from irony, 37
Ridicule, 3, 5, 38
Rigidity, 3, 5, 38
Rumor, 96

Sarcasm, 3, 5, 38, 39
    difference from insults, 39
Satire, 3, 4, 5, 39–42

Subject Index

Scale and Size, 3, 5, 42
Scenery, 48
Schlamatzls, 49
Schlemiels, 49
School for Scandal, 3, 9, 12, 13, 14, 37, 45,
Senex figures, 9, 49
Seventh Seal, 33
Shakespeare and the Ends of Comedy, 82
Similes, 13
Slapstick, 3, 5, 42, 63
Sleepers, 23
Social Significance of Humorous Techniques, 111–113
Speed, 3, 5S, 42
Stereotypes, 3, 5, 42–44

Techniques of Humor
  dominant and secondary, 4
  forty-five techniques, 1–50
  in Miles Gloriosus, 58, 59
  play frame and, 4
  social significance of, 111–113
  used on combination, 4
Theme and Variation, 3, 5, 44, 45 46, 49, 83–96, 108
Tragedy
  relation to comedy, 115

Transformation, 8
Travesties, 6, 7, 25, 26, 27, 30, 31, 33, 34, 36, 41, 42
Trickster figures, 20
Twelfth Night, 3, 23, 24, 28, 29, 31–33, 49, 65–82
  abuses of logic in, 68–70
  closure in, 82
  importance of appearances in, 72–74
  mistakes in, 72–74
  names of characters, 67
  problem of identity in, 71, 72
  problem of status in, 75
  wordplay in, 67, 68

Understatement, 4
Unmasking and Pretense, 3, 5, 45, 46

Verbal irony, 27
Vested Interests: Cross Dressing and Cultural Anxiety, 75, 76
Voice Usage, 47
Volpone, 8, 9, 10, 11, 23, 24, 27, 60

Wild Strawberries, 33
Wit, 34, 35
Wordplay, 58, 67

Zuricher Post, 36